Kitty Litter:
Thoughts from the Heart

Kitty Kaye

Front Cover Illustrated by
Debbe Femiak

Kitty Litter: Thoughts from the Heart
By Kitty Kaye

Registered with Writers Guild of America, East, 250 Hudson Street, New York, NY 10013

Printed in the United States of America

*Dedicated to the trials of life
which, though they often
cause us many tears and pain,
polish off our rough edges
and make us smooth as
tumbled stones.*

Table of Contents

FOREWORD

Life can be challenging. I don't think anyone would argue with that statement. When I was little, my mother always told me there would be days like this. However, she didn't tell me there would be so many of them!

From the struggles of raising children through the conflicts of trying to find meaning and purpose to our lives, this thing called life keeps us constantly wondering: *Why does life have to be such a battle? Do kids ever grow up? Will things ever get better? Am I spinning uselessly around in circles? Does any of this ever end?*

Kitty Litter: Thoughts from the Heart has two goals. One is to reassure you that you are not alone. We all face similar struggles and challenges in life. The other is to encourage you to look on the bright side. Through every trial, there is always something to be learned, a ray of hope in every battle, a rainbow at the end of each storm. Yes, the storms of life will come, and they will go. Sometimes they might leave an aftermath of destruction for us to deal with. But the skies will eventually clear, the sun will return, and life will move on. And somehow we will forget most of the pains of the past and find that what we have left are many cherished memories. And those precious memories are what give life so much meaning. So – chin up! Let's do this thing called life.

The Art of Living

The Art of Living

ABOUT THE ART OF LIVING

Life is a funny thing. We can set our schedules and make our plans, only to find out that life has an agenda of its own. Life doesn't wake up in the morning and consult with us about what we want to do for the day. It just takes off, does its own thing, and often leaves us running to catch up!

There are a lot of ways we can react when life doesn't behave the way we want it to. We can pout and be mad. We can yell or scream, maybe even throw something across the room to make us feel better! But what does it solve? None of that really does much to improve the quality of our lives.

The stories in *The Art of Living* are geared at helping us find humor in the grievances of life (as hard as that may seem at the time) and learn to find satisfaction in the simple pleasures of life. It's true that not one of us is guaranteed of a tomorrow. That makes it extra important to enjoy the humble gratifications of today and not let the little things overwhelm us.

Some of these stories are written just for fun. There isn't necessarily anything to be learned from them, just silly thoughts about life itself and the art of living it. Life is what it is - sometimes silly, sometimes frustrating, sometimes beautiful, but always unpredictable.

Whatever the case, it's important to remember that we are the main elements of life. It is up to us to help each other through and find ways to enjoy the many blessings we have. Stay positive, and laugh along with life. Be thankful each morning when you wake up, just knowing that you have been blessed with another day. After all, if you woke up this morning, then God must think you are still qualified to run this race called life. Hop out of bed and give it the best you have to offer! And never let it get you down, even when it doesn't follow your game plan!

A CHRISTMAS GIFT

It was a few days before Christmas, and I was pleasantly surprised when I arrived at work and found an unexpected gift on my desk. I took the delicately wrapped item out of the gift bag and removed the tissue paper. It was a sweet, little angel ornament, so I immediately hung it on my computer monitor so everyone could see it. Since the gift bag was hardly used, I decided to take it home and save it for another present.

At home, I told my husband about the unexpected gift and what a nice thought it was. He asked who it was from, and I replied that I assumed my coworker who sits next to me had left it on my desk. Remembering that I still had the bag with the tag on it, I decided to check to be sure.

Imagine my surprise when I looked at the tag and realized the gift was not even intended for me! It was from the coworker I suspected, but she had left it on the wrong desk! I quickly stuffed the gift bag back into my purse to make sure I didn't forget to bring it with me in the morning.

The next day, I arrived a little earlier at work in an effort to beat my coworkers. I promptly removed the angel from my monitor and re-wrapped it in the tissue paper, relieved that no one seemed to have noticed the error. Before any of my coworkers showed up, I hurriedly placed it on the proper desk. And when the appropriate coworker opened it up, I donned a look of surprise and complimented her on what a beautiful ornament it was.

I didn't tell her that it was slightly used, and fortunately for me, she hadn't noticed that I had one just like it hanging on my computer monitor the day before! Next time, maybe I will check the tag a little closer before making any assumptions!

A LITTLE TOOT

It was one of those days. I should have just stayed off the road, and called in sick. I wasn't a mile from home, and had already had to dodge two gray squirrels and a black crow standing in the road. The crow appeared to be snacking on one squirrel that hadn't made it! Then a little further down the road, a car pulled out in front of me, only to promptly stop right in the middle of the road with no warning. I wondered if my car was either invisible or had a sign on the front of it that read: PLACE DENT HERE!

But finally, I was on the home stretch. There was just one more intersection before I could pull into the parking lot at work. However, as I got closer to the intersection, I could see the car in front of me was not moving, even though the light was green.

This traffic light was known to be short-winded. It usually allowed about two and a half cars through before it turned yellow, and he had already wasted enough time for one. I am not typically an aggressive driver, but with all I had already been through making it to this point, I just wanted to pull into work and not sit needlessly waiting for the traffic light to go through another cycle.

I was driving a Mustang, my muscle car, so I decided I would just pull up behind him and blow my horn. I expected a blast that would propel him through the intersection, or at least show him how much power my car had. Instead, all I got was a little toot!

What was that? I chuckled to myself. I was expecting a masculine blast, and all I got was something that sounded more like a little chickadee tweet! But it was enough to get his attention, so we both made it through the intersection in time. And the little toot brightened my day. Instead of walking into work grumpy from the hassle of my commute, I walked in laughing about the masculine car with a horn that goes toot!

A SIMPLE APOLOGY

My husband and I had to run some errands after supper, and it had taken a little longer than expected. Now it was dark, and we still had one more stop to make before we could head home. We pulled into the parking lot of the last store, and my husband opted to stay in the car this time. I told him I would be right back, and headed across the parking lot.

Since it was winter time as well as nightfall, I focused on the ground as I walked, watching for icy spots. Slipping and falling in the parking lot was not something I was interested in doing. Suddenly, I realized there was a moving vehicle getting dangerously close to me. He was headed in my direction, and he didn't seem to be slowing down. In fact, I was beginning to think he was aiming for me!

Since he didn't seem to be stopping, I did instead. I stood and stared at him in disbelief as he sailed by me and into a parking spot. Apparently he wanted that particular space, and he didn't care if he drove over me to get to it. I was stunned at what I considered to be dangerous and disrespectful driving skills.

I gave him a dirty look, muttered something under my breath (or did I really say it out loud?!) about rude drivers, and continued my trek into the store. A few minutes later, the driver of the car in question walked in and saw me standing there. I was still stewing, wondering if I should tell him what I thought of his driving abilities. But before I could say a word, he surprised me.

He was a young man, probably in his early twenties, and appeared to be the kind you might expect to misbehave behind the wheel of a car. But he stopped, looked directly at me, and said, "Sorry about what just happened. There was a glare from the lights, so I couldn't see you walking across the parking lot."

I assured him it was fine, since everything had turned out okay. He then smiled, nodded his head, and walked away.

Now what would the outcome have been had he not

stopped and given me a simple apology? I would have been upset about it all night long. I would have gone back to the car ranting and raving about the lunatic that almost ran over me in the parking lot. And I would probably have told everyone I talked to about the rude driver I had encountered. Yet it was not at all what I had thought. He wasn't a lunatic or rude. He simply hadn't seen me due to the glare.

I think that sometimes we make an apology bigger than we need to. We feel we can't apologize until we come up with the right words, or the perfect place to apologize, or find the ideal situation. Or perhaps we might stew about a situation long enough to decide that it isn't up to us to apologize. However, the quicker we apologize, the easier it is. Plus it can clear up any mistaken situations.

I'm glad that young man took a moment (and that's all it was) to apologize. It changed my whole outlook on the incident. Instead of thinking poorly of him, I was impressed with his character. Sometimes a simple apology can go a long way!

A STITCH IN TIME

We've all heard the old proverb, "A stitch in time saves nine," and I'm sure it's true. It makes perfect sense. If you stitch a hole in time, it will save it from getting bigger. But the bottom line for me is that I just plain hate to mend!

For years, I was very good at getting my mending done. Every time I found something with a hole in it, I ran it through the laundry, folded it up, and put it neatly in a pile. When the pile got big enough, I would take it to my mother's house so she could mend it for me! She loved to sew and, being retired, it gave her something to do. But those days are gone.

So now what am I supposed to do about the holes in my clothes? I don't have a sewing machine, nor do I have time to sit down and mend them by hand. I'm sure I have a needle and thread somewhere, but I'm just not sure where it might be. And who thinks about buying supplies like thread at the store? Not me, anyway.

My husband bought me a blouse awhile ago that came with a hole in it. He usually checks clothing thoroughly to make sure there are no holes before he buys them, but this one got past him. And my thought is simple - it came that way, so it stays that way!

It's not that I am lazy. It's the time factor, or lack of it! Now the funny thing is that I used to work as a seamstress when my kids were little. I had an industrial machine and sewed diligently every night until bedtime. But I think the difference lies in the fact that I was being paid for that sewing. No one pays me to mend my own clothing.

I recently put on a pair of my favorite pants while dressing for work and realized the seam had split. I really wanted to wear them, so I found an effective method of mending. I grabbed a package of safety pins out of the cupboard and went to work. It was a successful mending job, if I do say so myself. I just hope none of the pins let go when I sit down. That could be painful!

Since then, the safety pin mending method has worked

very well on other garments, too. However, I'm going to have to stock up on them if I keep it up. Once they make it into the seams of my clothing, they seem to stay there!

So as far as the "stitch in time saves nine" theory, I think safety pins work just as well!

PS I recently found my sewing kit, which contained needles and spools of thread, so I sat down to mend some clothes while watching television. And you know what? It's not anywhere near as dreadful a chore as I thought it would be! And it's cheaper than buying safety pins. Probably safer, too!

ABOVE REPROACH

My grandson thought he was being helpful. I was giving his brother a bath, and he was cleaning the bathroom sink.

"Look, Grandma," he said proudly. "I scrubbin' the sink."

If he was scrubbing the sink, there wouldn't have been a problem. But he was actually scrubbing the countertop, and that was a problem. My countertop is a wooden one, and by scrubbing it with the bathtub scrubber, he was actually taking a layer of polyurethane off.

I quickly jumped up and took the scrubber away from him. As I checked the counter to see what the damage was, he crumbled onto the floor in a defeated heap.

I hadn't meant to make him feel bad. I just knew that it would be a lot of work to fix it if he had scratched the finish off. And I also knew Grandpa would not be happy.

I comforted him and reassured him that he was just trying to help. He hadn't meant to do anything wrong. Then it hit me that as human beings, we want to be above reproach. We don't want someone to burst our bubble and bring us crashing down. We don't like to be corrected, scolded, or reprimanded. Something in our flesh just cringes when we are berated. We want to be above the criticism, above the repercussions of doing something another person might perceive as amiss or inappropriate. Quite simply, nobody likes to be wrong!

But the bottom line is that we are all human, and we will always make mistakes and be subject to the criticism or disregard of others. We can like it or leave it, but it will always follow us throughout our lifetimes. No two people think alike, and our actions are sometimes going to be misread, unappreciated, or corrected no matter how genuine they might be.

So don't give up just because it seems as though your efforts weren't appreciated. Keep on scrubbing. Just make sure you don't take the finish off!

ACRONYMS

My coworker and I at one point used a lot of acronyms to get us through some difficult times. We were going through a massive office transition, and it was not going well. Not at all! Every time we would have a meeting to discuss issues, we would leave more frustrated than before. We just had too many changes to deal with, and no clear solutions to any of them.

I found the only way I could get through the meetings successfully was to write some acronyms for myself. So on a little sticky note, I wrote IDRM (It Doesn't Really Matter), DLIBY (Don't Let It Bother You), and KYMS (Keep Your Mouth Shut!). It proved to be beneficial (somewhat), as every time I got frustrated, I would look at my sticky note and try to remind myself it didn't really matter. Of course, the acronym I had the most trouble with was the one about keeping my mouth shut. We all know how the tongue likes to wag!

After those meetings ended, we still used the acronyms. When we gave each other birthday cards, we would write acronyms in them and then try to figure out what they meant. Not only was it fun, but it proved useful to us. She had a particular issue that she was dealing with, so I wrote an acronym for her that she posted on her computer screen. It was our little secret as to what it really meant.

Well, as time moved on, so did we. She has left the company, and I have transferred to another department. One day, I was having a hard time with a lot of stuff going on, most of it personal dilemmas. I felt completely defeated, so I decided to write myself an acronym that would encourage me when I looked at it.

So here is what I came up with – YGTMI, K. Do you have any guesses what it might mean? It simply means – You're Going To Make It, Kitty.

When you are down and out, maybe it would be helpful for you to create some acronyms of your own. No one needs to know what they mean but you. Then hang them someplace where you will see them frequently, and remind yourself that EWBO (Everything Will Be Okay!)

ALL IN A NAME

At work, I spend most of my day entering data on the computer. It can be tedious work that doesn't consume a lot of brain power, so my mind sometimes wanders. Looking at all the different names I see throughout the day, I often come up with some comical combinations. Here are a few examples of some of the fun names that could exist.

If Sarah Black was to marry Robert White and they hyphenated their last names, they would be the Black-White family. There would be no shades of gray there! And if Bethany Good married David Horsey, they could be the Good-Horsey family. Just think of all the little cowboys they could raise!

Then there is Rebecca Wall and Charles Street. You've got it – they would be the Wall-Street family and could raise a bunch of little brokers. And if Jessica Nim married George Rod, they would have a family full of Nim-Rods. There could be a Bird-Bath family, and a Rock-Roll family of musicians.

The May-Day family would always be in a state of crisis. The Snow-White family could give birth to a bunch of little guys. And the Joy-Anger family would probably end up with personality disorders. Then if Chloe Bigg married William Butts, well, we aren't even going to go there…!!! And if Jenny Hamm married Mitchell Berger, they would be the Hamm-Berger family!

I love the name game! There is just no end to the humorous combinations you could come up with. But I think my all-time favorite hyphenated family name is this one: If Michelle Hacker was to marry John Wacker, they could be the Hacker-Wacker family. And if they had a son and named him John, Jr., they could tell everyone that this is their son, little Johnny Hacker-Wacker! I love it!

So if you have a plain name like Smith or Jones, maybe you should be thankful. There is a beauty in having a simple last name! Our pastor always says different is good, but in some cases, basic might be better! It's all in a name or, in this case, a combination of names!

BEING THANKFUL

The challenges of today may sometimes seem overwhelming, but always stop to be thankful for the blessings as well. There is always something to be thankful for. And the thing to remember is that life can change at any moment, so it is important to be appreciative of what we have.

When our children were younger, we lived beside a brook. Our bedroom was on the back side of the house near the brook. It was always so relaxing during the summertime to have the windows open and listen to the bubbling flow of the brook. It was such a soothing sound. I was appreciative of the sound as it lulled me to sleep every night.

However, during one particular storm, that brook became a raging wall of water. A culvert located a few miles above our house washed out, causing a wall of mud and muck to flow down through the valley. On that Sunday morning, we woke up having everything we needed to make us comfortable in life. We fled when we heard the flood was coming, and returned an hour later to find that we were homeless. The water had picked our house up, only to drop it back down again, leaving it broken and uninhabitable.

It was a life-changing experience. Prior to the flood, my kids would whine and pout if they couldn't get a material item they thought they simply couldn't live without. After the flood, I needed only to remind them of their blessings in life to redirect their thoughts. Having slept on their grandparent's floor for five weeks until we could find another place to live, they knew they had nothing to complain about. They were satisfied with having their basic needs met – like food, a bed to sleep in, clothing to wear, and a house to call home.

In today's society, it's easy to think we need all the new, modern gadgets and technology to make us happy. But sometimes all we need is family, a home, love, and to have our basic needs met. So, if you are able to say you have such things, don't forget to be thankful for them. Life is unpredictable and has the ability to change at any moment in time. You can wake up in the morning having everything you need in life, and go to bed homeless. So, don't overlook your blessings in life. And always remember to be thankful! Little blessings go a long way.

BROWNIE BATTLES

Brownies are so delicious, especially when they are still a little gooey on the inside. I will admit that I love to eat them, but I hate making them. I have just never had good luck with it. They either turn out dry and hard, or they are too gooey to get out of the pan. They never seem to come out just right.

While I was at the store recently, I saw a box mix and decided to try it. Maybe that was the answer I needed, just avoid making them from scratch. I was so excited that I bought a couple of mixes and headed home. I was sure I had found the secret to making the perfect brownie.

As soon as I got home, I mixed up a batch and threw them into the oven. I carefully set the timer for the exact amount of time, not wanting them to be undercooked or over-cooked. When the timer went off, I took them out and let them cool. However, they still seemed too gooey in the middle, so I put them back in the oven again.

After about an hour of popping them in and out of the oven, I decided they had to be done. When they had cooled for the last time, I successfully removed about half of the brownies and put them into a container, but I couldn't get the rest of them out of the pan. Believe it or not, they were still too gooey. How could they not be thoroughly baked with all the time they had spent in the oven?!

I had had about enough of these brownies, and I was determined to not be defeated by them. They were coming out of that pan, one way or another. I got my spatula out, and went to work. However, I pushed down so hard it broke the handle off! And when it did, it knocked the container of brownies off the counter and onto the floor! And, of course, it landed upside down! Talk about frustrating!

I guess it's better than what my friend did, though. She threw a batch of brownies into the oven, and then promptly forgot they were there. By the time she remembered them, they were terribly burned. I told her that she hadn't made brownies, she had made blackies! Unfortunately, she didn't see the humor in my comment. Oh well, at least I now know that I am not the only one who has trouble baking brownies!

Anyway, that does it for me. I am done making brownies! The next time I see a bake sale with brownies, I am stocking up on them. I will just put them in the freezer and thaw them out when I want one!

P.S. A great thing happened recently. My son married a girl who knows how to make brownies. Now I am set for life! Every time I want brownies, I can call or text her and drop a hint. She can be my official brownie baker!

CHANGING TIME

It has often baffled me as to why people feel they need to change the time. Why is it important to change the clocks an hour ahead in the spring, only to put them back an hour in the fall? What purpose does it really serve? Is there anything that we really gain from it? Or is it best to just let nature take its course and leave the clocks alone?

Now, I will be the first to admit that I really don't mind changing the clocks in the fall. It gives me pleasure to set them back and get an extra hour of sleep. But spring is another story. I feel cheated when I have to go to bed and lose an hour of sleep.

One might think that maybe I should plan better, knowing that we will lose that hour, but it just doesn't seem to happen. Even with the best of planning, I still find myself going to bed at the same time (which is really an hour later after I finish changing the clock!).

Once when I was a child, someone miscalculated and changed the clocks too early in the season. It was still pitch dark in the morning when it was time to go to school. I remember walking to school in the darkness, feeling like I should still be at home in bed.

However, that isn't as bad as what happened with our family one other time. That particular time, my mother couldn't remember if she was supposed to set the clocks ahead or back. She discussed it with her sister, and they came to the conclusion that the clock was to go ahead one hour. So, they both set their clocks ahead and went to bed.

In the morning, they got their families up and dressed, then headed to church, only to find the place deserted. As it turned out, they were supposed to set the clocks back, and we had all gone to church two hours early! We definitely didn't have to fight for a parking space that morning!

If my vote mattered, I would say to just leave the clocks alone. Mother Nature knows what she is doing, so let her do it. Then your children wouldn't run the risk of walking to school in the dark, no one will lose an hour of sleep in the spring, and you won't go to church two hours early because your mother messed up!

FEED THE BIRDS

Looking out the sliding glass door in the dining room, I noticed the bird feeder was empty again. Since there was still snow on the ground, I knew the birds would probably appreciate if I put some food out for them. Being full of good intentions, I poured some bird seed out of the bag and into a container to bring outside. But before I could get out the door, I was interrupted.

Two days later, the container of bird food still sat on my dining room table. I just couldn't seem to find the time to take it out to the bird feeder. Part of the problem was that I didn't want to trudge through the snow in the morning when I was wearing dress shoes, ready to head to work. And by the time I got home after work, it was already dark outside.

Finally, one morning as I was putting my coat on, I glanced out the window and saw a dove sitting on top of the birdhouse. It was facing the sliding glass door, and I swear it was watching me in an attempt to make me feel guilty about the empty bird feeder. I really didn't want to trek through the snow and go to work wet and cold, but I didn't want the birds to go hungry either. So I did what any kind, thoughtful, hard-working, busy, running-behind person would do. I slid the sliding glass door open and threw the birdseed out on top of the snow!

There, now we were both happy! The container was empty, so I didn't feel guilty about not feeding them. The birds would now have something to eat, they would just have to pick through the snow to find it. So we both won! A win-win solution!

But here is something to consider about this whole situation. Sometimes we have good intentions, but that isn't always enough. The container of bird food was useless to the birds as long as it sat on my dining room table. They could stare at it through the window from their perch in the bird feeder, but it couldn't alleviate their hunger.

We need to do more than just think about doing good

deeds. We need to act on our intentions, even if our approach isn't quite the quality we want it to be. Sure, it would have been better if I actually put the bird food in the feeder, but at least by throwing it out the door, the birds were able to access it!

So put some action behind your good intentions. No one knows the helpful thoughts or ideas you might be harboring inside unless you put them into motion and make the effort to share with those in need.

HELPING HANDS

Recently I had a couple of experiences that opened my eyes about being helpful. I had a friend who was having trouble keeping up with some of the things she needed to do, so I decided to lend a helping hand. I didn't ask if she wanted any help, though. Instead, I just stepped up to the plate and tackled some of her workload. I hadn't meant to offend her, but apparently that is what I did. She felt I had overstretched my boundaries and tread on her territory.

Her response caught me a little off guard. I wasn't trying to step on any toes, nor was I implying she wasn't capable of managing her duties. I had only intended to lend a helping hand since she was having such a busy day and mine didn't seem to be quite as hectic.

A few weeks later, a similar situation happened to me. My grandchildren had made a mess in our row at church. They had strewn paper, wrappers and tissues on the floor where we had been sitting. I had fully intended to clean the mess up before we left. When my kids were little, I had always told them whoever made the mess got to clean it up. Since we had made the mess, it was naturally our responsibility to take care of it.

However, while I was helping my daughter put coats on the kids, a man sitting nearby came over and started picking up the mess. At first, I was offended. Did he think we were actually going to leave the church a mess? I knew it needed to be cleaned up and planned on tackling it just as soon as we were done with the children.

Then I thought back to that day when I had unintentionally upset my friend by offering help that she hadn't asked for. Maybe he was doing the same thing. He saw that we were busy with the children, and he was just trying to be helpful by cleaning up our mess.

It is funny how we can sometimes be defensive when there is no reason for it. So here's something to ponder: If it appears someone is trying to help you out, don't take it the wrong way. Be appreciative of the help and simply thank them for caring enough to lend a hand. After all, there isn't one of us that couldn't use a helping hand at some point in life.

LESSONS ON LOVE

While listening to the radio, I heard a discussion in regard to the meaning of life. Did you ever stop to think about it? What exactly is the meaning of life? Why are we all here on this earth rubbing shoulders with each other? If you never left your house, would anyone even know you existed? What would be the purpose of being alive?

I allowed myself to mull it over for awhile as I drove home. I was so deep in thought, I paid little attention to where I was going. I hope I obeyed all the traffic laws! Anyway, by the time I got home, I had finally come to a conclusion, and I'm sure you will agree.

It isn't the size of your bank account that defines life, or the amount of money you have managed to stash away in your piggy bank. It's not your position at work, making life more meaningful when you're at the top. It isn't defined by the number of friends you have, although that is important. No, I say the bottom line is that love, and how you share it with others, has got to be the baseline behind the meaning of life. Without love, life seems so pointless, meaningless, and ultimately hopeless.

Now it's helpful to consider that there are different kinds of love. There's that initial love and respect you feel for your parents as a young child. Then there's the powerful, knock-your-socks-off kind of love that consumes your whole being when you meet that special someone you've been waiting for all your life. And then there's the overwhelming, words-just-can't-describe kind of love that engulfs you the first time you look into the eyes of your newborn child. And, of course, there's the all-encompassing love that only comes from above to give you peace and reassure you that life is good.

We are all born with an innate ability to love. And maybe we don't have a special someone to love at the moment, or have never given birth to a child. However, we all belong to a family, or community, or society as a whole where we can love, cherish, and play an active role.

Love is what makes us belong, whether we are kin or not. Love makes the world go around. So love your spouse, your children, your family, your community, and your country. Even if you are housebound, you can still reach out and share some love. Send someone a card or a text to let them know you are thinking of them. Pick up the phone and call a friend. Or maybe make a donation to a charitable organization. Be an active part of life and enjoy its purpose, because if you don't have love, you're missing out on the most important piece of life. In fact, you would miss the very essence of life itself.

LETTERS TO MYSELF

I'm not afraid to tell people when they have had a positive effect in my life. When someone has done something nice for me, something that is beneficial to me or touches my life in a special way, I always try to be sure to thank them. It may be in the form of a card, a phone call, or a special little gift. I just want them to know how much I appreciated their thoughtfulness.

And then there's the other side of me. Just as I articulate my thanksgiving, I sometimes speak out in frustration. If someone does something that upsets me or causes me some form of discomfort, I'm apt to share some thoughts about it. It is hard for me to keep quiet and tolerate it in silent agony. And this can be a problem, especially if the 'someone' causing me the discomfort is my boss or my husband. In such cases, I usually regret voicing my concerns. I might stand the risk of losing my job, or spending a sleepless night on the couch!

So what's to be done about the other side of me? How do I keep that side from speaking out and causing further discomfort? Well, I have a few ideas. Maybe I should just give myself a time-out. I have always found time-out to be effective. Just go take a breather, get my thoughts and emotions together, and then come back in a better frame of mind.

Or maybe I could go for a nice, brisk walk. If I am really upset, maybe I could even try running. No – I guess I never get that upset! I was just not born a runner, and I never will be one! Being athletic has just never been a part of my chemical make-up. Better to stick with the brisk walk.

If none of the above works, I can always write. As you can tell, I love to write. So when the other side of me feels the need to speak out, I think I can successfully do it in the form of writing. That way I can get it off my chest and out on paper. But then, taking it one step further, I will just outsmart myself and mail the letter to myself instead of the party who has offended me! That way I will be the only one who knows about that other side that can sometimes get me into trouble! And by the time the letter arrives, I will probably have gotten over whatever it was that I was upset about to begin with.

Yes, I do believe that is the perfect solution to the problem! And knowing how I feel the need to voice my opinion, added to the fact that I like to write, I think I better invest in some paper and stamps. It could become quite a project. And if I do mail the letters, it would probably be wise to not put a return address on it. The post office might think I'm nuts writing letters to myself all the time!

However, now that I think of it, mailing them would probably not be a wise decision. It would cost too much, for one thing, and the post office might wonder why my volume of mail increased. So instead, I can just put them in a file labeled LTM (and I'm sure you can figure out what that stands for!)

LIFE'S CHALLENGES

I had high hopes for the day. There was a project I had been working on for years, and it was close to fruition. I had spoken with someone who could make my project come to life. We had made plans to meet on Saturday morning, so I packed up my paperwork and headed her way.

However, when I pulled in, I didn't see her car in the yard. There were no lights on inside, and when I tried the door, it was locked. Had I misunderstood? I thought we were both on the same page about when and where to meet.

I sighed in disappointment, but knew the project could wait. I had already been working on it for several years, so another week or two wouldn't hurt. I would just give her a call later and find out what had happened. But I still felt discouraged. I had been so excited about taking the next step.

Looking across the road, I saw a thrift shop. So as not to make this a completely wasted trip, I decided to go check it out. Maybe I would find something fun and exciting to lift my spirits.

It was a very nice thrift shop, and I did find a lot of things I wanted. But as I got to the check out counter, I groaned when I saw the sign. NO CHECKS WILL BE ACCEPTED. Arrgh...I hadn't brought any cash with me since I didn't plan on going shopping. So I would just have to write this one off as a wasted trip.

On the way home, I stopped to pick up a couple of kids. It was Earth Day, and I thought it would be fun if we participated in the local clean up. We stopped at my house for lunch first. They asked for Spaghettio's, but when I looked in the cupboard, I couldn't find any. I asked what their next choice was. They said macaroni and cheese with hot dogs. I looked for a macaroni and cheese dinner, but also came up empty. Guess it's time to go shopping!

Determined to not be defeated, I made homemade macaroni and cheese and warmed up some hot dogs. There, success at last! We gobbled our lunch down, grabbed our bags, and headed out to pick up trash. But if I thought things were going to go any better than the beginning of my day, I was only fooling myself.

They were very excited about the thought of helping out with Earth Day, and eagerly picked up the trash they came across. But it didn't take long for them to lose interest. My bag had gotten snagged on a piece of brush and had ripped almost the full length of it. While I was trying to figure out how to salvage the bag, both boys wandered off into the park.

I called several times to them, but they were more interested in playing than helping me pick up dirty trash. I could still see them, but didn't feel ambitious enough to chase after them. Yet, it soon became apparent that calling was not going to convince them to come back. I would have to go retrieve them. By then, I decided we had had enough fun picking up what little trash we had, so we headed home.

When we arrived back at my house, I saw my husband had left the mail on the table. I opened one of the letters, and was surprised at what it said. Apparently this agency had been misinformed about a situation, and had incorrect information on file. As a writer, I determined I would just have to write back to them and set things straight. But then I remembered my previous article about speaking out when I should keep my peace. So I decided if I do write to them, I will address the letter to myself until I could get a little peace about the issue and handle it properly!

Then my mother called and said a relative was having problems. It was a topic I had written to this person about and, in my effort to help, I think I might have only made the situation worse. (Maybe it was one of those letters I should have mailed to myself?!) Anyway, it seemed I had only made things worse instead of better. I felt truly defeated, like I was just not winning.

Finally, the day was over and I decided to go to bed. As I tried to climb into bed, I somehow managed to get tangled up in the sheet and blankets and had to struggle to get myself out of the mess. There were two questions that came to mind – "*Will this day ever end?*" and "*Does everyone have as many challenges in life as I do?*"

I finally made it into bed and laid my head down on the pillow. I allowed myself to reason things through and came to the conclusion that other people do have just as many struggles. Some of them are plagued with painful medical conditions. Some of them have cancer. Some of them are in abusive situations. Some of them have been abandoned, or are homeless. And a lot of them have much bigger problems than all the little things I had dealt with today.

Life is a challenge, but there is always something positive to think about. Just having breath in our lungs and being alive for another day is something to be thankful for. And it helps to always remember that things could be worse. So sure, I had some challenges today, but I survived. And tomorrow, I'm sure I will have more. But you know what? I'll get through all of them somehow, too, just like we did today! It's not so much the challenges of life that matter. It's how we handle them that counts.

LOSING YOUR LUSTER

Years ago, my husband and I built a house. It was quite a project, but we enjoyed working on it together. We designed it on paper, and then carried it through to fruition. He was unemployed at the time, so during the day, he would put a wall up. I would come home from work that night and put a coat of polyurethane on the wall he had just constructed. And that's how we built the entire house – one wall at a time.

I often look around our house and smile with satisfaction. Not only am I pleased with the final product, but I can honestly say I know every inch of our house, since it was my job to coat each board with a layer of protection.

That may have been years ago, but the house still looks great. The boards on the wall have changed color with time, gradually growing a shade darker year after year. However, there is one board that always catches my attention.

As I walk down the steps into the basement, there is a face board over the top of the stairs that has never dulled with time. Maybe being sheltered from the sunlight has allowed it to keep its original color. I'm not sure what the reason may be, but it's just as beautiful today as it was the day we put it up there.

I know I think way too much, and often put meaning into inanimate objects, but as I walked past that board today, I couldn't help but think how I want to be like that board. I don't want to ever lose my shine, or let the harshness of life dull my outlook.

I know as I age, my physical body will get old and wrinkled, but I hope my spirit keeps its luster. And that is my wish for you as well. Don't ever lose your luster or zest for life, no matter how weathered you might sometimes feel!

MANAGING STRESS

Stress is not a fun thing to deal with. I think we would all agree with that. Do you know how I handle stress? Not well! When it comes to managing stress, I fail miserably. I just don't always have the ability to let it go.

So when I get stressed out, here is what I sometimes do: I yell, or moan and groan, rant and rave, or do a lot of griping. And as I mentioned before, I write myself letters when I am upset about something. When I am stressed, I sometimes write so much I get writer's cramp! And I probably speak out way more than what my husband appreciates!

I think it's just that I want others to understand my frustration. Perhaps I am just looking for a little empathy. Whatever the case, when I have adequately vented, I feel really bad that I have. I regret the things I have said and done, and wonder why I couldn't just keep my mouth shut and my thoughts to myself. (And as we all know now, it's because I don't handle stress well!!)

There came a time when I had to sit back and take a tally of my life. I clearly wasn't happy with the way things were going. Stress had become my way of life, and I didn't like what it was doing to me. And I'm sure no one else enjoyed it either. But was there anything I could do about it?

After analyzing it, I realized there were a couple of things I could do. I am the kind of person that wants to do it all, wants to be involved in everything and not miss any opportunities. Because of this, I found I had taken on more than I could humanly handle. I never had a chance to sit down and rest. I had constant demands on me, or something that always needed to be done. So even though I didn't really want to let go of my involvements in various community organizations, I knew I had to. And then I took it a step further and made a career change.

Do you know what happened? I found that I was much more relaxed, and I wasn't verbalizing my frustrations as much. I actually started to like myself again! And I think my family likes me better, too! Plus no more writer's cramp from writing so many letters to myself. It was better in almost all aspects.

I will admit that I do miss the involvement in the community organizations, but maybe I will pick and choose what I can do in a guarded manner so as not to overwhelm myself again. Maybe just take some baby steps and take on small projects. I wouldn't want to get myself stressed out again (and believe me, neither does anyone else around me!)

MY OLD BLAZER

Walking through the parking lot at work was a lot like walking around the show area of a car dealership. There were shiny sedans, polished sports cars, and huge pickup trucks. Each of them seemed to be well maintained and fairly new. But when I got to the old Blazer with the rusty fenders, I unlocked the door and climbed inside.

I looked at the odometer, and it read over 270,000 miles. I knew I didn't have the money to purchase a new vehicle, so I had decided I would just keep driving this one until it wouldn't go anymore. For a moment, I allowed myself to sit behind the wheel of the old car and have a little pity party for myself.

As I did, I felt God speaking to me, and He had some legitimate questions. "*When you turn the key, does your Blazer start? When you need to go somewhere, can you count on your Blazer to get you there? Do you spend a lot of money on car repairs? Is your Blazer frequently at the garage?*"

We both knew the answers to these questions. This Blazer had been the most dependable car I had ever owned. It hardly ever needed repairs, and the fact that it had close to 300,000 miles on the odometer was a testament to itself. I had never owned a better car.

I started my Blazer with a smile on my face. As I drove off through the parking lot, I felt a sense of pride in my car. On the surface, it was still a rusty, old Blazer, but I couldn't have been any more pleased than if I was driving a shiny, new Cadillac. All those rust spots were just beauty marks, earned by years of dedicated service!

And I have since learned how to deal with the embarrassing noises my rusty old Blazer can sometimes make. I simply roll up the windows and turn the radio on. It's a simple solution, and a great way to make the squeaky noises disappear!

OBSTACLES IN LIFE

It had been one of those mornings. Nothing had gone right, and I had faced one obstacle after another in my effort to get to work. And to top it all off, when I finally got there, someone had parked in my normal parking space.

At first I was upset, but then I realized I had a choice to make. I could pout and be mad that someone had the nerve to park in my space, or I could simply ignore it and find another spot. It would be one thing if the space was labeled with my name, but it was not. And, on a more realistic note, I was going to be late if I didn't park soon.

As I walked into the building, I contemplated how we face many obstacles in the course of life. It is our choice how we will handle these obstacles. We can jump over them and hurdle them like an Olympic track runner prepared for the challenge. We could break them down violently, similar to a thief breaking in where he doesn't belong. We could choose to quietly avoid them and walk away without making a fuss. Or we might simply choose to lie down in front of our obstacles and give up. The choice is ours. And just as we control the decision, our choice determines the outcome.

Realistically, we sometimes just don't have what it takes to always hurdle our obstacles. We would need to keep ourselves in a constant state of preparation. There is no question that life's obstacles can wear you out. However, there's nothing wrong with taking a little breather from the challenges. Give yourself a day off. Or if you don't have the ability to take a whole day off, at least find some time when you can stop and relax for a bit.

I have heard it said that time-out isn't necessarily an effective method of discipline when training children. However, I disagree with that. I have found, even as an adult, sometimes taking a time-out is just what I needed. And then, when I am refreshed, I can go back and tackle the problem with renewed strength and vigor.

So don't be afraid to take a time-out to regroup and

regain your stamina when your obstacles in life become too challenging. But don't lie down in front of your obstacle and fall asleep. Remember the story of the tortoise and the hare. A sleeping runner goes nowhere!

POPCORN, AN AMERICAN FAVORITE

Last night we went to the movie theater. The movie stunk, but the popcorn was great! We got there a little early, and it gave me a chance to watch other people before the movie started.

A couple of aisles away from us, I saw a man chomping away on his popcorn. His technique was just like mine. He was eating it just as fast as his hand could get it from the bucket to his mouth. I smiled and thought, "Ah, now there's a man after my own heart!"

Believe it or not, we ate the whole bucket of popcorn before the movie even started! I told my daughter that now we could focus on the movie instead of the popcorn. I will admit that I felt kind of foolish getting up to throw the popcorn bucket away before the movie had even begun, but then I bumped into another man doing the same thing! All right – someone else who eats popcorn like me!

Can you imagine how boring movies would be without popcorn? It would be like a baseball game without hot dogs, or peanut butter without jelly. Movies and popcorn just seem to go together. Our family jokes that we don't necessarily go to the theater to see the movie anyway. We go for the popcorn. And for some reason, it just doesn't taste the same at home. My family always popped our own popcorn when I was a kid, and I make homemade popcorn frequently for my kids. However, I just can't make it taste as good as theater popcorn. It's not bad, mind you, just not the same.

So thank God for inventing popcorn. It makes it worth sitting through some of the boring movies my kids like to go see!

RAINY WEATHER

It was another rainy day – dark, cloudy and wet. We had encountered a string of them lately. There had been so many, it was getting depressing and hard to remain upbeat. I knew the sun would return some day, but when?

At times, life can be discouraging like that. We sometimes get stuck in an emotionally rainy season. Everything seems gloomy and cloudy, and we wonder if the sun will ever return. Simply functioning during these dismal days can be a real task. But a change of mindset might be helpful in many ways.

While rain may not be as enjoyable as a bright, sunshiny day, it certainly has its purpose. What a boring world it would be without rain. Flowers would wilt and lawns would turn brown. Gardens would fade away and rivers would dry up. Ultimately, it is the rain that adds color to our world, making the grass green and the flowers such a beautiful sight. And a gray day always makes the colors look brighter. Somehow the green leaves and colorful flowers seem so much prettier against a dark background.

So when you are stuck in a rainy season of life, put your raincoat on and go play in the rain puddles. Enjoy the cool rain, and try to see it as refreshing. Keep yourself occupied until the storm passes. Remember that there's a silver lining behind every dark cloud, if only we are willing to look for it. Find meaning and purpose through each storm, as hard as it might be. Maybe God has something for you to gain from this experience.

So while you search for that silver lining, allow yourself to have some fun splashing in the puddles. Remind yourself how important the rain is to the very element of life itself. And always remember that the dark clouds won't last forever. There is an element of beauty to be discovered in every day, and something beautiful lurking behind each cloud.

THE DASH HOLE

I received an unexpected blessing a few years ago – a little Mustang sports car. It's not that I have a special interest in Mustangs, but it is a cute little car that I would never have bought for myself. I have always had vans, or sedans, cars that were large enough to hold lots of kids for my child care business or family. The Mustang came as a surprise.

At the time, I had a seven-passenger Dodge Durango that had just been sitting idly in my yard. With my child care business closed, and my kids grown and out on their own, it wasn't a vehicle I needed anymore. I was having trouble selling it as gas prices had been high, and no one wanted a car that swallowed a lot of gas. So there it sat.

One day, my son stopped by and asked if I would like to trade it for a Mustang. He had a friend who needed a bigger car, as their family was growing, and he knew I wanted a smaller one. So it was a match made in Heaven. We traded vehicles, and both walked away feeling like the winner.

I was content with the Mustang as it was, but my son decided the stereo system needed upgrading. He purchased a new system and installed it, but found it didn't fit the same. After the installation was complete, there was an open hole in my dash. The new system just wasn't designed the same as the one it had replaced.

It was an unsightly hole, too. I could see wires hanging down on the inside of the dash. I asked what he was going to do with the hole, and he said his friend would try to find an aftermarket pocket to fill it. But month after month went by, and still I had a dash hole with visible wires.

I just couldn't take it anymore. So I did what any true redneck would do. I found a tissue box that was the same color as the interior of my car, trimmed it to the right size, and then stuffed it into the hole! It looks pretty good, if I do say so myself! And it's a good thing it does, because it has been a couple of years now and I still haven't seen any aftermarket pockets coming my way!

So you can call it Yankee ingenuity or a true redneck solution. Either way, it works for me. And the cost fit my budget, too! A win-win situation!

THE LAST SUPPER

Cars lined the driveway, and people were everywhere. Our family members from across the country had come to visit. It had been a long time since we had seen them, so we had invited all the local relatives over for a massive family gathering. It was a busy scene, and proved to be an amazing event.

We were having a cook-out, and everyone had brought food. A row of tables held the salads, chips, vegetable and fruit trays, and plenty of desserts. A couple of grills were smoking with delicious smelling scents wafting out of the vents. The food looked delicious, and the awesome smell of meat grilling made my stomach growl.

It was nothing short of a wonderful experience. The children were running around playing ball. Their laughter brought a smile to my face, as did the jovial sounds of the adults laughing and talking. And those long awaited hugs felt so good.

I watched silently for a spell, trying to store up all the sights and sounds in my memory. I realized that there is nothing that can replace family. You have a common link, and no matter how long it has been since you have seen each other, there is familiarity and a bond like no other.

I would have liked for this day to last forever. However, as the saying goes, all good things must come to an end. And so it did. Sooner than I had hoped, the party broke up and everyone headed their separate ways.

Within a matter of months of that blessed day, one of the family members was diagnosed with lymphoma. Then another acquired a different form of cancer. A couple of the elderly relatives died simply from the complications of old age. In a decade or less, many of them were gone. Unfortunately, we had all been so busy with our lives, we hadn't had a chance to get the whole family together again.

We had a wonderful time that day, but didn't realize it would be our last complete family gathering. Had we known how quickly some of our loved ones would pass, we might have spent more time together. We just assumed there would be more beautiful days ahead of us, and plenty of time to get together again.

Yet, life waits for no one and time moves swiftly. So cherish those family gatherings. Spend as much time together as possible, filling your lives with good food and time spent with family. One never knows when you will have had your last supper together.

THE RUSTY YEARS

All of my life, I have heard talk about the Golden Years. You know the years I mean. A time of leisure and rest, and not having to get up every morning to run out the door for work. A time to be free to do what you want, when you want, and where you want. However, I'm now beginning to think it is only a myth that abides in the minds of middle-aged working folks, some kind of fantasy that helps to get them through each day.

As I age, I find my memory is not what it used to be. My memory has always been keen, allowing me to do well in my school days. But now, if I don't write myself a note, I won't remember what I am supposed to be doing. You should see all the sticky notes located throughout my house. Notes on the kitchen table, notes on the refrigerator, notes attached to the strap of my purse so when I get my car keys I'll remember what I need to do.

Speaking of car keys, it's amazing how much time I spend looking for them. If I remembered to put them back in my purse, I'm good to go. If not, I could spend the next half hour looking for them. In my younger years, I worked for a middle-aged woman who could never find her car keys. At the time, I wondered what was wrong with her. Now that I am middle-aged, I understand all too well!

Not only does your brain function change, but your body does, too. You can tell yourself you are still young, but a body knows the difference. I made the mistake of sitting down on the floor to play with my grandchildren. One of them needed me to get up and help him, and I couldn't believe what a difficult task it was. Struggling to make my way off the floor, I kept thinking I must look like a beached whale trying to get back into the water!

A relative of ours recently wrote to me, telling of all her aging woes. She said she thought the Golden Years should be renamed. The Rusty Years would be much more appropriate. I'm beginning to agree with her! There is nothing 'golden' about a body that doesn't function properly anymore! Rusty joints and dented fenders are a better description of the human body in the latter years of life!

TRY, TRY AGAIN

For most of my adult life, I had wanted to go to Atlantic City. It's not that I am a gambler. It's quite the opposite, actually. I'm more afraid of losing money! Atlantic City just seemed to hold some kind of fascination for me. I wanted to walk the boardwalk, see the sights, and follow the streets that have the same name as the Monopoly game.

Then one year, in celebration of my birthday, we decided this was the year we were finally going to make it to Atlantic City. We packed the car and headed out. The first day, we stopped at my sister's house and spent the night. The next morning we went out for a birthday breakfast. However, on the way back to her house, it became quite clear that we were not going to make it to Atlantic City.

It wasn't a long drive from the restaurant back to her house, but it was far enough for the car to malfunction. As we pulled into her yard, we groaned in dismay at the steam pouring out from under the hood.

My heart sunk. I had been so excited about finally visiting Atlantic City, yet it didn't look like it would happen during this vacation. My husband, being a mechanic, did what he could to fix the problem and we decided to head home. We packed up and turned the car back toward the direction from which we had come.

However, after driving for about an hour, we realized the car seemed to be functioning fine. Not wanting to give up on our vacation so quickly, we set our sites for a northerly destination. We had always wanted to go to Lake George, NY as well, so we headed that way. We spent the night in Lake George and, since the car still seemed to be in a cooperative mood, we headed even further north. I had always wanted to go to Lake Placid as well, so away we went.

That was the strangest vacation. We ended up having a wonderful time. Both Lake George and Lake Placid were beautiful, and we have returned to Lake George multiple times since then. Apparently, the car just didn't want to go to

Atlantic City that week.

My desire to go to Atlantic City never faded, though. And here's the funny thing. We connected with a group in the area that does a bus trip to Atlantic City twice a year, so we have gone multiple times since that first failed attempt. In fact, the last time we went, one of the gift shop owners recognized us because we had been there so many times!

This makes me think of a story about my mother. Her dream destination had always been Niagara Falls. When she and my father got married, they almost made it to Niagara Falls on their honeymoon. However, my dad got tired of driving and gave up before they made it. So for their 50th Anniversary, we decided to take them to Niagara Falls. (It only took us fifty years to get our act together!)

It would be a family trip with not just my parents, but also a couple of my sisters and some of our children. We planned the trip for April so we wouldn't have to deal with bad weather. However, Mother Nature thought she would be comical that week, and we had a late season blizzard! We had planned it for the week of school vacation so the kids wouldn't miss school, and we had all rearranged our work schedules. It seemed like it would be challenging to reschedule it, so my mom was ready to throw in the towel. She said she wasn't meant to go to Niagara Falls. It just wasn't in the cards for her. Thanks for trying, but don't worry about it.

We weren't going to give up that easily, though. It had taken us fifty years to come this far, and we couldn't call it quits now! So my sister made some calls, we rearranged the plans, and brought our parents to Niagara Falls on Mother's Day instead. And what a wonderful time we all had. It was a family vacation to remember.

This reminds me of an old saying that my mother used all the time – "If at first you don't succeed….." Well, you know the rest!

UNEQUAL ROLES

Sometimes I feel as though I have a heavier work load than my husband. He comes home from work and sits down in his recliner to watch television. And that is where he stays for most of the night, right up until bedtime. I, on the other hand, come home from work to make supper, clean the kitchen and wash the dishes after supper is over, and then go to work on the laundry. When I am done with the laundry, it is time to pack lunches for tomorrow. By the time I am done, it is time for bed and I am exhausted. How is that fair?

Then add to that the complication of having children. Why is it that woman get to go through all the work of bearing children? Dealing with the morning sickness, weight gain issues, and all the pain that comes with giving birth? Men just sit back and watch the whole process. And after the child is born, it is usually the women that are up at night for the feedings and changing the dirty diapers. The men can roll over and go back to sleep.

I can sometimes have a real pity party for myself, but there are times when I can sit back and bask in the role of being a female. One of them is when it starts to snow. And then I can say, "*Honey, the sidewalk needs to be shoveled after you are done plowing the yard.*" Another time is when the wood box is empty, and I can say, "*Honey, can you go get some more wood for the stove, please?*" Or if I am having car problems and the car is making an unusual noise, I can say, "*Can you check my car out? I think something needs your attention.*"

I have to admit the snow issues have the greatest impact. I can stay inside and wash my dirty dishes while my husband is outside dealing with the nasty, frozen, white stuff falling from the sky. And that's when I really don't mind being a woman. My place is inside where it is warm and cozy! And if I could shut my conscience off, I would be tempted to sit in his recliner, pick up the remote, and find a nice, sappy movie to watch. So why don't I give it a try....

I found sitting in his recliner to be quite comfortable. It's not a place I have often had the chance to sit, since it is usually occupied, but I could now understand why he sat there so much. I decided to wrap myself in a blanket, and then picked up the remote to see what was on TV. It didn't take long to realize that I didn't know how to manage the remote. He had always made it seem so easy, but then he has had a lot of experience with it!

However, two problems quickly occurred. I couldn't find anything worth watching, or that wasn't a rerun, and then my conscience kicked in. He was out in the freezing cold weather, dealing with nature's harsh elements, and I was wrapped in a blanket, snug as a bug, while sitting inside in his comfy recliner. Man, why did I have to be born with such a sensitive conscience?!

I told myself if I was a good wife, I would find a shovel and make my way outside to help him. But then I came to my senses and realized somebody's got to wash all those dirty dishes and do the laundry…!!! And experience has taught me that if I don't, it will all sit right there and wait for me!!!

USE YOUR WORDS

My daughter was instructing her young son to use his words if he wanted something. Simply pointing at it was not enough. He needed to learn to verbally express what it was that he wanted. Being a writer, I had to stop and think about the importance of words. What would we do without them? Wouldn't the world be a boring place without words?

The words we need to communicate are a vital part of life. What would society be like without the ability to talk to each other? Or write to each other? Cell phones would cease to exist, there would be no television or books, and we would probably all sit around the campfire and grunt at each other like cavemen!

Words are so important, and shouldn't be kept to ourselves. If there is someone you feel is very special, don't forget to let them know what they mean to you. If someone has done something extra nice for you, reach out and let them know how much you appreciated it. If there is someone in your life that you wouldn't want to live without, make sure they know what an important role they play in your life. How will they know if you don't tell them? Pointing and grunting just doesn't do the trick!

So come on, cavemen, stop your grunting. Pick up your pen and write a note. Or grab your cell phone and send a text message. Or maybe even give someone a call. Don't let those unspoken words float loosely around in your head. They won't benefit anyone but you in there. You need to speak up and share those thoughts. Just think how much better life could be if you use your words to encourage others and let them know you care.

WHEN PEOPLE ARE EXASPERATING

Sometimes people wear you out. It happens to the best of us, even if you are a people person and love the social life. One day recently, I came home from work so worn out that I told my husband I didn't know if I even liked people anymore. It had been a day when I had been yelled at consistently by irate customers. It wasn't necessarily that I had done anything wrong. Yet, I was the unfortunate recipient of their wrath, whether I deserved it or not. If I had done something worthy of their punishment, that would have been one thing. But all I wanted to do was help, even though my efforts didn't seem to be appreciated.

When you get to the point where you don't know if you like people anymore, it's time to take an inventory of your life and determine what the problem is. Have things been accumulating, an ongoing series of occurrences that leave you burned out and frustrated? If so, maybe it's time to make some changes, like a career move or an adjustment to your daily routine.

However, it might only be an occasional occurrence that just happens once in awhile. Perhaps the full moon or the season changes play a part in people's moods. If you like what you do and realize these days will happen randomly, maybe it's worth sticking it out. Everyone has a bad day, customers and employees included.

Whatever the case may be, you don't want to give up on people as a whole. Yes, there are those individuals who will never be satisfied with what you do, no matter how far you bend over backwards to help them. But that remains their problem, not yours.

If you want to restore your belief in the goodness of people, maybe you should get involved with your community. But that is dealing with more people, you might think. That is true! But it is in a charitable way that will make you feel good about yourself, and might help renew your belief in people. Plus it will take your focus off yourself and help shed some happiness into the lives of others.

For several years, I have hosted community events in town for the local children. It is sometimes an Easter Egg Hunt, or sometimes a Tree Lighting Ceremony at Christmas time. While they are a lot of work, it is a special feeling just to see the joy it brings to the children. Or there are lots of other community groups that you could get involved with – Boy Scouts, Girl Scouts, church groups, etc.

If you don't have time for meetings, maybe you could sponsor a needy family in your neighborhood. There are always families that could benefit from a little TLC from others. And volunteering your time helps you see life from a different perspective. It gives you a level of satisfaction that you might not always find at your place of employment. Working is something we do to pay the bills, but volunteering is something we do for fun or to improve the quality of the lives around us.

If you are burned out from dealing with people, allow yourself some time to figure it all out. Whatever the case may be, don't lump all people together and get sour on them. There are those who will always be a challenge to deal with, but I believe there are a lot of good people out there. And it is people (and our interactions with them) that make life worth living. So don't give up on them as a whole. Find your fit in society, and learn to love people – even the exasperating ones!

ENDING THOUGHTS ON THE ART OF LIVING

Okay, so life is full of setbacks. We all know that, and we have all experienced them. Some of them can be catastrophic – like death stealing away a loved one or a special pet, or losing your house to a fire or flood. Life is a series of setbacks, full of changes, and can be compared to seasons and changing of times.

Unfortunately, there is no avoiding the challenges. When the earth shattering tragedies hit, they will knock us right off our feet. It takes time to recover from those situations. We need the time to heal and recover, then struggle back up onto our feet and figure out how to move forward.

More often, though, our setbacks will be little things like "*Where did I leave my car keys now?*" Or "*Why is traffic always backed up when I'm in a hurry?*" or "*Why can't anything ever be simple?*" And it's the little things that wear you out and get on your nerves. It's easy to become frazzled when time after time you have to deal with problem after problem. When will it ever end?

But life is a journey, full of seasons and changes. Sometimes the sun is shining, the weather is beautiful, and life couldn't be any better. Life can be warm and exciting, like the brilliant blue sky and golden sunshine of summer. But then sometimes the rain clouds roll in and it pours for days, making us wonder if we will ever see the blue sky again. Sometimes life is bright and colorful like flowers in a garden, and sometimes we are stuck in shades of gray, like the bleak days of winter. Sometimes we are on the mountain top and life is great, but sometimes we seem to be roaming aimlessly around in the valley and can't seem find our way out.

So here's the bottom line. That's life! Life is going to be challenging and a series of ups and downs. I don't want to burst anyone's bubble, but no one ever assured us life would be easy. There's no reason why it can't be fun, though. There are a lot of good things in life. Life is packed full of wonderful things, special people, and beautiful places. And we are meant to enjoy each and every one of them.

I think the best way to survive life (successfully, anyway!) is to accept that life will have a multitude of upsets. Some of them we will be able to plan and prepare for and some of them we will not. Some of them will catch us completely off guard and we will find ourselves totally unprepared. But through it all, the important part is to not give up on the belief that life is good. Its suitcase full of ups and downs can be difficult to lug around at times, but we need to stay optimistic, find our way through it, and move onto better times.

If you are in one of those times where your suitcase is too heavy to carry, just drag it along behind you for awhile. But remember to remain focused on the positive, accept that the negative things will happen, and stay strong. Believe in the beauty of life. You may not be able to see it at the moment, but that doesn't mean it doesn't exist. Keep moving forward, and search the horizon. You will get there. Somehow, someday we will all make it through this thing called life. And when we do, I'm sure we will find many happy memories packed away in that suitcase!

I am not a therapist, but here is some advice for you. Sit back, relax, and breathe. Life is going to happen, so just go with the flow and don't sweat the small stuff. If you wear yourself out on all the little things that go wrong, you won't have the energy to take on the big stuff. So keep a smile on your face, keep your chin up, and determine to be happy!

Oh, and don't forget to be kind to each other. After all, people and how we treat each other is what life is really all about, right?! Love is the true meaning and the foundation that supports us throughout life. So don't just exist. Live, love, and learn the true value to the art of living!

The Joys of Parenting

The Joys of Parenting

ABOUT THE JOYS OF PARENTING

If you are a parent, you know how challenging it can be just to get through life one day at a time. We never know what a day will hold, or what new adventure lies around each corner. It sometimes feels as though life itself has become nothing more than a game of survival. Often we are trying to outsmart time, and always struggling to do more than is humanly possible in less than an adequate amount of time. As if that isn't enough of a load, we also deal with behavioral issues and constant disciplining, while often trying to stay sane through it all.

The Joys of Parenting section of this book is a collection of events which I jotted down throughout my children's youthful years. They are not necessarily in chronological order. In fact, they tend to bounce back and forth from early childhood to adolescence. Yet, if you are a parent, this probably will not be a problem for you. Parents somehow become accustomed to bouncing...!! And some of the stories pertain to experiences as a grandparent. However, it is all still a part of the parenting process.

None of these articles were written as a means to vent or complain. It is understood that parenthood is a demanding role and takes stamina to do it properly. Instead, these articles are intended to encourage the parent and help them know they are not alone. We all have times when our children have pushed us beyond our physical and emotional limits, causing us to say or do things we wish we hadn't. Let's face it – none of us are superheroes. We all have a certain level of human tolerance and perseverance.

The main intent of these stories is to help you learn to laugh off those frustrating experiences that really make you want to pull your hair out! Read these articles as written by a mother who has been there and understands the challenges you face. And keep in mind that kids will grow up – eventually!

As parents, the best we can do is to keep our chins up and carry on. Yes, I have found that children do grow up and move out. However, if you think your troubles will end when they do, you are only fooling yourself! Yet sooner than you realize, you will look back and grasp how quickly the years disappeared, and might actually miss the days of active parenthood. So in the meantime, love your little ones and don't let those seemingly never-ending, day-to-day trials get you down.

A BEAR OF A DAY

It seemed like such a simple plan. I had promised my kids I would take them to the Build-a-Bear Workshop at the mall. They were very excited about the plan, but the day turned out to be a challenge right from the very start.

That morning, I woke up with stomach cramps and felt terrible. But I didn't want to disappoint them. We had been talking about this trip for weeks, and I knew how much they had been looking forward to it. So I had some toast for breakfast, packed some ginger ale and crackers to bring along, and off we headed.

We hadn't gone far when I realized it was just going to be one of those days. The needle of my gas gauge was on empty, as usual, so I told the kids we would need to stop and get gas. However, everyone seemed to be in slow motion, and I was worried we would run out of gas while we sat and waited in traffic.

We got to the first gas station (and yes, we had to try more than one) only to find that the credit card system was down. So I had to try another station. After I filled the car, my gas tank appeared to be dripping. So I went to get my cell phone and call my husband to see if it was okay to continue, but no cell phone! So instead, I drove back home to have him check the car and also retrieve my cell phone.

By this time, I was already exhausted, and we hadn't even made it out of town yet! My husband checked the tank (which, of course, was not leaking and made me look like a paranoid mother!) so we continued on our way. Heading up over the mountain, we got stuck behind a big truck going a whopping 10 mph with no passing zones. Since it had taken so long to get this far, we decided to just stop in the next town for lunch and also get away from the truck we had been stuck behind.

The next problem was that we stopped at McDonald's at the wrong time, and it was full. One of the kids wandered off and when I went to go get them, we lost our place in line.

So it took an extended length of time to get our food. By this time, I was so discouraged by the way the whole day had been unfolding, I just wanted to give up and go home.

But then it was suddenly as though the test was over and we had scored well. The day seemed to take a turn after lunch, and the rest of it went great. The kids had an awesome time at the Build-a-Bear Workshop, and came home proudly toting their new bears. They couldn't wait to show Daddy what they had made.

So what was the lesson for the day? I don't know – maybe perseverance pays off?!! Don't give up because victory is just around the corner? Whatever the lesson, my kids didn't remember any of the bad parts. All they told their father was what a good day it had been, and they didn't put their bears down for days. So thank goodness I didn't give up because of such a rough start. Those bears, and my children's pride in making them, made the 'bear' of a day worth all the frustration!

A HAPPY BOY

My son loves tools. When he was only three, I bought him a set of plastic tools. He promptly told me that he didn't want plastic tools. He wanted metal ones, just like Daddy. So when he turned four, I bought him a few metal tools so he could start his own collection.

One day while we were in my husband's workshop, he found a couple of old electrical hand drills in a pile. It appeared they were being discarded, so I asked if it was okay for him to play with them. Daddy said that was fine, as he was planning on throwing them out anyway.

I gave them to our young son, and you would have thought I had given him a pot of gold. The fact that they no longer worked didn't seem to matter to him in the least. He had "real" tools like Daddy, and that's all he cared about.

He walked around the yard for quite awhile, carrying a drill in each hand, almost as though he was on a mission. Or maybe he was trying to figure out what to do with them now that they were his. He was most likely looking for a project to tackle, but maybe didn't even know what the tools were used for. Whatever the case, I couldn't help but smile, and also take a picture or two.

After watching him for a short time, I smiled and said out loud, more to myself than anyone else, "Now there is a happy boy!"

He turned, looked up at me with an element of surprise on his face, and asked, "I'm a happy boy?"

"Yes, you are," I said, ruffling his hair.

Then I thought how comical it was that he had to be told he was a happy boy. But maybe we could all benefit from that once in awhile. Maybe if no one else does, we need to stop and remind ourselves occasionally that we truly are happy, too. And sometimes all it takes to make us happy in life is to give a little boy two hand drills that don't even work! It sure put a smile on my face, and his as well!

A LION IN THE WOODS

He wanted to go for a walk in the woods, and being a four year old child, nothing I said could dissuade him. It's what he wanted to do, and I could join him, or he would go on his own. The problem was, I really wasn't interested in joining him. I was tired and had too many other things to do.

So off he went, heading into the woods alone. I grew desperate and knew I had to do something to stop him. So I called out to his departing back and said, "Watch out for the wild animals. They can run faster than you because they have four legs and you only have two."

He just kept walking and never slowed down. I accepted my fate and decided I was going for a walk in the woods, but decided to let my husband know where we had disappeared to. I hurried over to the house to call into him, and then rushed to catch up with the wandering woodsman.

When I got to him, I was surprised to see that he hadn't gone far. He heard me coming, and turned around to face me.

"Did you see that?" he asked.

I hadn't seen anything, so I asked, "See what, honey?"

He pointed off into the forest and said, "That big animal."

I looked in the direction he was pointing, but saw nothing.

"What animal?" I questioned him.

He searched the woods with wide eyes and said, "It was a big one." He paused, and then added, "I think it was a lion."

I turned my head quickly so he wouldn't see me smile. I didn't want him to think I was laughing at him. I'm sure we don't have any lions in the woods around our house, but I won't tell him that. If he fears the lions in the forest, he won't wander off into it and get lost.

"I think he is gone now, sweetie," I reassured him. "He probably went home to check on his family."

"Oh," he said quietly, and then added, "Let's go home, too."

Yes, a win-win situation. He learned fear and respect of the unknown, and I don't have to go for a walk in the woods. Someday I will tell him there are no lions in the woods, but for now, I will let the thought keep him close to home. It might sound mean, but at least he won't wander into the woods alone for awhile.

A QUICK TRIP TO THE STORE

Okay, so if you have ever gone into a store with a child, you will be able to relate to this experience. It was supposed to be a quick trip into the grocery store just to grab a loaf of bread and a gallon of milk. However, when you enter a store with a child, there is never anything "quick" about it!

The first thing he spotted was the candy rack. In fact, it was almost as though it was a magnet, drawing him right over to it. I told him no candy, it was almost supper time. Then he noticed the cooler full of soda, strategically placed beside the check out counter and candy rack. Again, I reminded him that it was supper time.

Amazingly enough, he didn't give me too much trouble about it. We made it to the bread rack, where I picked up a loaf. Then I quickly grabbed the milk and we headed for the check out counter. Yet, if I thought we were going to get out of the store that easily, I was only fooling myself.

On the way to the check out counter, I made the mistake of passing by the display with all the Easter candy on it. Oh my goodness! Before we were done, I was beginning to wonder if we would be home by bedtime, not talking about supper time! And probably, as most kids would, he picked the most expensive, useless item there – and that was what he wanted! In fact, that was all he wanted!

I tried to convince him to settle with one of the inexpensive chocolate bunnies, or some jelly beans, or maybe a cream-filled Easter egg. But oh, no – he wanted a big, plastic Easter egg that lit up and changed color. What good was that?! He would probably bring it home, plop it in the middle of the dining room table, and promptly forget it even existed. And I didn't need a big, ugly, plastic Easter egg in the middle of my table. Plus it cost too much money. At least if he got some candy, he could eat it. That had some use to it.

So I'm sure you have an idea about what came next. First, he insisted it was the only item there that he wanted. Then he crossed his arms and refused to budge. He didn't just cross his arms, though. He wrapped them around the Easter egg so I couldn't take it away from him.

At this point, when all else has failed, a child will usually start to cry or at least make enough noise to create a disturbance. And what is a mother supposed to do then? If you give in, you have just taught them that if they want their own way, all they need to do is cry and make a big scene. (I hate to admit it, but it always seemed to work for me as a child. Maybe that is why I am so determined to not let it work for my kids!)

Finally, after what seemed like an hour or two (but was probably just a matter of minutes,) I convinced him to get a bag of rainbow cotton candy. Not that I wanted him to have cotton candy either, but I wanted to get home and make supper. I explained he couldn't open the bag until later, and wondered if I should have just let him get a candy bar when he had first asked. Maybe I could have saved myself the battle at the Easter candy display!

He tucked the big, ugly, plastic Easter egg onto the back of the shelf, hoping no one else would see it and buy it. (As if anyone would want it anyway!) And as soon as we were in the car, he started asking when we could go back and buy it.

"Will you have enough money for the egg when you get paid?" the little voice in the backseat asked. "I hope it's still there when we come back."

But here's the thing – I think the next time we go back, it isn't going to be "we." It will be just me, unaccompanied by any kids. He can stay home with his father!

A WINTER COOK-IN

Winter time can be so dreary. Not only is it cold and stormy, but the color is gone. No colorful flowers or green grass to brighten the day, and even worse, no trips to the beach or park. Life is black and white, and unless you like to watch television or play out in the cold snow, it can be quite boring.

One particularly bleak January morning, I decided I would pretend it was summer time and fake a barbeque. I took some chicken out of the freezer to thaw, and then whipped up a potato salad, along with a fruit salad while I waited. When it was closer to supper time, I coated the chicken with barbeque sauce and popped it into the oven. My mouth watered in anticipation.

I grew anxious for supper time and found it hard to wait. To make it feel more like a picnic, I got out some paper plates and napkins. I even brought out a few bottles of soda and paper cups. However, I held myself back when it came to the red and white checkered tablecloth and the plastic silverware.

When the "picnic" table was set and supper was finally ready, I called the family out to the kitchen. I was sure they would be as excited as me when they discovered we were having an indoor cookout, but wow, was my bubble about to burst.

My son sat down at the table and literally looked at his plate with disgust.

"You know I don't like the kind of chicken that has bones," he complained.

No way was I going to let his sour attitude spoil my picnic. I sweetly smiled and replied, "Sorry, honey, but that's all I had."

He poked and prodded at his chicken, clearly displeased with is meal. "Not much meat on here," he continued to complain. "Guess I'm gonna hafta have some ice cream for dessert!"

My daughter has never been much of a meat eater to

begin with, so she didn't even poke at her chicken.

"If you don't want your chicken, have some potato salad," I suggested.

"I'm not eating that!" she firmly stated, "It has eggs in it!"

She finally satisfied herself with a large helping of fruit salad.

However, it became quite obvious that no one seemed to be enjoying this meal like I was. My son had a friend over and, to add insult to injury, he proceeded to tell me the meal didn't taste as good as it smelled.

I tried to ignore it all and continued to revel in my meal, but it was apparent that I was walking this road alone. After dinner, I asked my husband if he had liked the meal. He shrugged his shoulders, not even looking up from the newspaper he was reading, and said it was all right.

Well, I guess sometimes you just have to do something for yourself, and that's what I told myself now. This meal wasn't for my family, it was for me! And I had enjoyed it, right down to the last bite. The beauty of it all is that I had lots of leftovers for tomorrow!!! And speaking of tomorrow, when it comes time for supper, I think I will serve beans and hot dogs! That will teach them to complain!

AVOIDING THE BEACH

We were just finishing up a great time at the beach, but when kids are involved, things don't always end on a happy note. I allowed my son to stay in the water while I picked up the toys on the beach, but now I wanted to leave. I was hot and tired, and ready to end this adventure. However, he was not on the same page. He wasn't coming out of the water, and that was all there was to it.

Have you ever been there before? What can you do when you have a child in the water that doesn't want to come out, and you are fully clothed and ready to leave? I'll tell you what I did. I did what any average, frustrated parent would do. I stood there and yelled at him, telling him if he didn't get out of the water right now, I would never bring him to the beach again. When he didn't respond, I added, "Ever!" – as if that would really make a difference.

And guess what he did? Absolutely nothing! He just kept swimming and ignored me. He knew I wasn't serious. He knew that coming to the beach was a fun, family activity that we all enjoyed and did frequently. To not ever bring him to the beach again wouldn't punish just him. It would punish all of us, including me.

So there I stood, red-faced and embarrassed at the water's edge, trying to figure out how to get this child to respond. In other situations, I might have put some distance between us, thinking he might fear being left behind and hurry to catch up to me. But I knew I couldn't do that here. He was too young to be in the water without close adult supervision. Plus, in this case, I didn't think it would work anyway. He was having so much fun in the water, he wouldn't have cared if I left town! So I did the next thing any frustrated, exhausted parent would do. I bribed him with an ice cream cone.

"If you come out right now, we will have time to get an ice cream on the way home. If you don't, we won't have enough time."

Fortunately, the bribe worked. But you can believe that

I will not let that become a habit. As soon as I got things settled down at home, I made up a chart for behavior at the beach. If he wears his life vest when he goes into the water and also comes out when I tell him to, he can get stickers. Once he has collected a determined amount of stickers, he can go shopping to pick out a prize.

And it's not a bribe – it's a reward for good behavior. Because we all know I can't avoid the beach for the rest of his childhood. I don't deserve a punishment like that!!!

CHUCKLES IN CHURCH

My daughter and I were passing notes back and forth in church. Now I know some would say that isn't appropriate, but it was keeping her quiet and entertained. And that is sometimes a difficult thing to do.

She passed a note over that said, "Are you having any more kids?"

I wrote back, "No way! Are you?"

She gave me a funny look, and then wrote back, "I'm too young to have kids."

Adding to the conversation, I asked, "How many do you want to have?"

She made a big, fat zero. It kind of surprised me, so I wrote a note asking her why she didn't want kids. She wrote back, "They are too noisy."

That's funny! Since when has noise bothered her? She was about one of the noisiest kids I have ever met. I had always thought girls were supposed to be shy and quiet. Maybe some girls were, but definitely not my daughter!

Then she must have started to get hungry, because the conversation turned toward the topic food. I could see her writing, and wondered what she was doing. She wrote, "What's for lunch?" and then made a list:

McDonald's
Burger King
Subway
Pizza

She wrote to check off "witch" one we were going to do. I hadn't planned on going anywhere after church, so I made an addition to her list.

Leftovers at home

I looked at her and smiled, and then she pointed to the instructions to check off the one we were doing. So I took the pen and promptly put a big, fat check mark next to the 'Leftovers at home' option. It struck us both as funny, and we started laughing.

However, we got caught in the act. The pastor heard us laughing and looked our way. He was probably thinking, "Did I say something funny?!"

Shame on us for fooling around in church! We will either need stop passing notes back and forth, or learn to muffle our chuckles!

CONVERSING WITH TEENS

Did you ever notice when teenagers are involved, life often seems to be just one argument after another? An easy request can become a heated argument. Here is a sample conversation that you might have with your teenager:

"You left the milk on the table. Can you put it away, please?"

He looks up from his cell phone, or whatever electronic device he might be playing with at the moment, and says, "You talkin' to me?"

You smile patiently and say, "Yes, honey, I am." And you think to yourself, Who does he think I am talking to – the dog?! We are the only people in the room.

He looks back down at whatever he holds in his hand and replies, "I didn't get it out."

You continue to be patient, stating, "But it's on the table right in front of you."

He never looks up this time, and just says, "Yeah, but I didn't put it there."

This conversation is starting to annoy you, and even though your patience might be starting to wear thin, you calmly reply, "Well, you probably used it, so you can do your part and put it back in the refrigerator."

He shakes his head in the negative and says, "I had soda."

It doesn't really matter if he used it or not. It needs to go back in the refrigerator, and there is no reason why he can't stop what he is doing for a few brief seconds to do what is being requested.

So you once more patiently state, "But it needs to go back in the refrigerator, so can you please just put it away."

He again fails to stop what he is doing or even look up at you and replies, "I'm busy right now."

Okay, so you've had about enough of this conversation. Maybe he didn't take the milk out of the refrigerator, and maybe he didn't leave it on the table, and maybe he didn't pour himself a glass of it, but there is no reason why he can't set his cell phone down long enough to put the stupid jug of milk back in the refrigerator! And does he not think that you are busy, too? It would be much easier for him to step away from the table long enough to put the milk away than for you to take your hands out of the soapy dishwater, dry them off, and do it yourself.

Your internal tea kettle has built up some steam, and you feel ready to whistle. So you raise your voice a little and sternly say, "I DON'T CARE WHO TOOK THE MILK OUT – JUST PUT IT BACK IN THE REFRIGERATOR! NOW!"

He looks up at you in stunned silence and, since you are on a roll, you add, "It would have been quicker to just do it than to sit there and argue with me!"

And then it hits you – that sounds just like your mother when you were a kid. Can it be true? Is it possible that you had conversations like this with your mother when you were his age?

Unfortunately, you know it's true! We were all teenagers once. But here's the beauty of it all. Your mother somehow survived your teenage years, and you will make it, too! And don't give in and do it yourself. Kids don't learn responsibility if mothers do everything for them. So stand your ground, Mom. He drinks the milk, sometimes, so he can help put it away!

DIRTY, OLD MAN

We all know that kids can be completely unpredictable with the things they say and do. As an example, I was in church with my grandson, and a man with disabilities was sitting a few rows in front of us. His disabilities had distorted his face and given him some unusual facial features.

My young grandson, who was sitting in my lap at the time, said, "He's scary!"

Fortunately, he said it quietly enough so that the man didn't hear him. I explained that we can't always help how we look, but that doesn't mean we can't be friendly with people who look different than us.

He nodded his head, as though he understood, and then immediately called out, "Hi, scary guy!"

Fate was on my side because 'the scary guy' apparently didn't hear the greeting. Or maybe he didn't think it was directed toward him because he didn't think he looked scary. Anyway, it reminded me of my younger days when my little sister did something similar.

My mother had stopped to buy some gas. Back in those days, the gas station attendant would pump the gas for you. If no one was available, the mechanic would come out to do it.

That was the case on this particular day. The mechanic's hands were extremely dirty from working on the cars, and my sister noticed it. While he pumped the gas, my sister asked if she could hand him the money when it was time to pay. My mother agreed, and rolled down the window for her, but then found herself so embarrassed a moment later that she wanted to crawl under the dash and hide.

As the mechanic came to retrieve the money, my little sister leaned out the window, gave him a sweet smile and said, "There you go, you dirty, old man!"

I always wondered what he thought of her comment that day. She hadn't meant anything deeper than what she had said. He was dirty, and he was an older man. But her comment probably didn't do much to improve the quality of his day!

There is no way you can prepare yourself for the things that come out of the mouths of children. One just never knows what to expect next! Their innocent comments can sometimes make your face turn multiple shades of red!

EASTER EGG GREED

The Easter Egg Hunt had been a success again this year. I had coordinated it for years, and this was the first year that no parents had complained because their child didn't get enough eggs. After all the hard work that goes into planning and preparing for it, I have always struggled with any complaints that came my way. After all, it's a free event, and taking home a few candy-filled eggs is leaving with more than they came with. I told my husband this had been the best Easter Egg Hunt ever, since no parents had complained.

Later that day, we went to an Easter Egg Hunt at the nursing home where an elderly relative resided. The toddlers were taken to a smaller, sheltered area for the hunt. Parents were given written instructions explaining that they were to make sure all children had at least ten eggs to begin with. After that, they could grab as many as they wanted. However, even though the instructions were quite clear, the rules were not adhered to. Some kids walked away with heaping baskets of eggs, while one of my little guys had nine in his basket and the other child had only five. Tell me that was fair!

We returned to the lobby of the building, and the kids sat on the floor to open their eggs. A mother and her children came in and sat right beside my kids. Her children were some of those with baskets heaped full with eggs, and they were excitedly opening them. I kept waiting for the mother to use some manners and tell her children to share some of their candy with my kids, since it was very clear that they had acquired much more. Yet sharing didn't seem to be a part of their game plan.

My children didn't complain. I'm not sure they even noticed that the other kids had a lot more candy than they did. However, I left disappointed and discouraged. Where were their manners? If the shoe had been on the other foot, I would have taught my kids a lesson on fairness and sharing by asking them give up some of their candy.

When I got home, my husband asked how everything

went. I asked if he remembered our conversation earlier that day about parents complaining when their kids don't get enough candy. Then I told him at the nursing home, I became one of them.

Now, I wouldn't consider myself to be a greedy person, and it wasn't greed that had me discouraged. I believe that sharing and trying to be fair is an important part of life, and that hadn't happened.

After today's experience, I know how it feels when things are not fair. But I did gain something valuable from this. I think next year I will bring extra candy for those who don't find as many eggs and, in so doing, try to guarantee that everyone leaves happy, parents included!

EASY OR NOT

We were in need of a new child care provider, and the search was not going well. I felt like I had spent the entire day on the telephone, trying to make a successful connection. But at the end of the day, it seemed that all I had gotten was a runaround with no clear solutions. Some of them didn't have any openings. Some had only part-time openings, and we needed full-time. Some could take one child, but we had two. Finally, I found one that could take both children full-time, but she required a substantial deposit before the kids could even begin attending.

I hung up the phone at the end of the day feeling defeated. Why did it have to be so difficult? Sometimes things are much harder than we expect or want them to be. Another day was gone, and I was no closer to a solution than when I had started this morning. Tomorrow would be another day, I reassured myself. I would just rest and pray about it tonight, then give it another try in the morning.

The next day, I was a little reluctant to pick up the phone and try again. I expected a repeat of yesterday, ending no further ahead. However, quitters never win, and I desperately needed to find a child care provider. The only way I would do that was to keep trying. So I dialed the first number on my list, and an amazing thing happened. I made a successful connection! She had full-time openings, could take both children, and didn't require a deposit. Why couldn't it have been this easy yesterday?

Perhaps at times we go through challenges to help us learn to be resilient. Sometimes the task is easy, and sometimes it is not. No matter what the case may be, we need to keep trying, keep moving forward, because there is an answer out there. And easy or not, those who are resilient are the ones who find it.

PS She turned out to be an awesome babysitter, too, and well worth the search!

GROUNDED FOR LIFE

At the age of four, my husband bought our son his first car – a battery operated Bigfoot truck. Our son was nothing short of ecstatic. It was a Christmas gift, and he had a hard time waiting for the snow to melt that winter so he could get outside and actually drive it. Hard plastic tires just couldn't get any traction on snow and ice.

When summer finally arrived, I thought he would wear the truck out. He drove it around and around, circling the yard over and over. When it came time to clean the garden out that fall, we put him to work. We loaded one pumpkin at a time into the back of his truck, and he drove them over to the house to put them on the porch. His favorite movie at the time was Chitty, Chitty, Bang, Bang, and he sang the theme song over and over as he drove.

However, he soon became overconfident as a driver. One day while I was working in the kitchen, he asked if he could drive his Bigfoot down to the garage to see Daddy. His father worked at the garage next door, which I could see from the kitchen window, but the road was much too busy for him to be driving his little Bigfoot on. I told him it was not safe, the answer was no, and thought that was the end of it.

A few minutes later, I looked out the window and something caught my eye. There was my son, driving his Bigfoot down the side of the road like he thought he was a real car! I absolutely freaked out! I was doing home daycare at the time and, with other kids in the house, I couldn't run out the door after him. So I quickly grabbed the telephone to call my husband and told him to go out to meet him.

Well, as you can imagine, he was grounded from using his Bigfoot for quite awhile. At first, I thought grounding him would not be an effective method of discipline for one so young, but it stayed with him for the rest of his life. When he misbehaved after that, I would threaten him with being grounded, and he knew the consequences.

To this day, he still remembers the time he got grounded for driving his Bigfoot down the road, even though he was so young. It didn't take much of a consequence to let him know the error of his ways. Just taking his favorite toy away for a brief period of time made him remember it for life! (And perhaps the way his mother freaked out had an impact, too!)

IMPORTANCE OF THE EARLY YEARS

When it comes to parenting, I think sometimes we fail to grasp how important the early years are. I have heard people say that you need to be careful not to spoil a baby. However, I tend to disagree with that train of thought. In my opinion, it isn't spoiling a baby to hold them, snuggle them, and attend to their needs. Let me share some thoughts about this.

I have worked with children all my life, in many capacities. I have run a child care center, provided both respite and foster care, and have worked in a residential home for teenage girls. I have adopted a child, and talked with a lot of other parents who have also adopted children. Through the years, I have come to a conclusion about child development and the importance of a child's first few years of life.

When a child enters life, they are eager to learn. They take in everything around them and begin to form their own philosophies. What they experience teaches them what they can expect out of life. If a baby cries because they are uncomfortable and someone picks them up to hold them or feed them, what are they learning? That their cry matters, that someone is there for them. What must a baby think when they cry and no one responds to them? That their cry doesn't matter? That no one is there for them? What a very sad thought.

A child who isn't showered with love and affection might develop the thought that they are not an important part of life. Or they might come to the rationale that they can do anything they want and no one will care. Or possibly they could foster an angry spirit, realizing that they cry out and no one responds to their need.

Babies and young children are so tender and vulnerable. As the responsible adult, it is our place to teach them that life is good, and that their existence matters. They are here for a reason. It is our role to show them love and reach out to meet their need, no matter how exhausted we might feel. Remember that they don't stay little forever. The next thing you know, they will be graduating from high school!

So can you spoil a baby by cuddling them, snuggling with them, and showering them with love? I say – No way! Bring it on! Let that little one know how important they are. It will help them to develop the philosophy that life is a good and that they are important part of it.

INTERRUPTED SCHEDULES

Everybody seemed to need something from me this week, above and beyond the usual, I mean. One child had a doctor's appointment. Another child had a dentist appointment. My husband needed me to run some errands for him, and I had an appointment of my own.

It all meant time away from my job. I was worried that my boss would be upset if I had to leave work, but she was very understanding. She had children of her own, and didn't mind as long as I worked as many hours as possible and got the daily work done. Thank goodness for an empathetic boss.

Even so, it was an exhausting struggle to try to rearrange my schedule to accommodate all the needs of my family. I spent the week racing from one place to another, feeling much like a chicken with its head cut off. (I have never really liked that saying. Poor chicken, anyway!)

As I drove home from my appointment, I had time to contemplate the week. As I did, I realized what an extremely lucky person I am. I had people (sometimes known as interruptions) in my life that needed me. They were people that counted on me to get them through and help them with their needs and problems. Isn't that what life is all about? People helping people, loving them enough to rearrange their busy schedules, and come to their aid when they need it? And these were not just any people. This was my family - my husband and children, the most important people in the world to me. They were worth every ounce of effort (or interruption) that I invested in them.

Having thought it through, now I am more accepting of schedule changes. I realize that sometimes my agenda will be challenging. Sometimes things will not go the way I planned, and I might find myself a little exhausted at the end of the week from all the juggling. Yet, I know that I am very blessed to have these wonderful interruptions (also known as family members) in my life. And I wouldn't trade my "interruptions" for anything!

JOY IN THE MORNING

It was finally the weekend, but that didn't mean I could rest and relax. Working full-time usually leaves me trying to accomplish more than I can handle during the weekend. Such was the case this week. My schedule for Saturday was full, but it was all about to fly out the window.

We started the morning by going out for breakfast. We hadn't driven down the road very far when I realized my plans were about to change. My car was making a loud noise, and I knew it couldn't be good.

We continued on our way and completed the breakfast plans, but my husband banned me from driving until he could fix the problem. How could I run my errands and accomplish everything on my To-Do list without a vehicle?

My heart was heavy as we drove home. Once we had arrived at home, I made the necessary calls to cancel my plans for the day and resigned myself to the boring task of housework. It was something that needed to be done, but I would much rather be spending time with the kids at the playground or running my errands that needed to be done.

By the end of the day, my house was cleaner, but my heart was still heavy. We didn't make it to the salon for haircuts, we couldn't go to the kids' favorite playground, and now I would have to squeeze my errands into my weekly schedule. I went to bed reminding myself of one of my favorite Bible verses, Psalm 30:5 which states, "joy comes in the morning." Tomorrow was another day. Hopefully, things would go better.

However, joy didn't come in the morning. Instead, vomiting and diarrhea did. I had a sick child. Yuck, what a nasty mess. I wondered how this could be fair. Two days in a row I would have to write off my plans for the entire day.

All was not lost, though. Later in the day, the sun came out and it was a beautiful day. I thought some fresh air might help my sick child feel better, so we went outside to play. It was a clear blue sky, and the bright sunshine made it feel unseasonably warm. We actually had a picnic and ended up having a wonderful time.

That night as I lay in bed, my heart was happy and overflowing. Maybe joy hadn't come in the morning, but it did finally come. It just arrived a few hours later than planned, and I had joy in the afternoon instead. And that fit in nicely with my motto, which has always been 'Better late than never'!

KEEPING THEM BUSY

Through the years, I had heard all the rumors and horror stories that come along with raising kids during the teenage stage. And I will honestly say that these were years I didn't look forward to. Would I be able to keep my children safe from harm and out of trouble during those challenging years? Would my motherly love and concern be enough to successfully guide them through? Would they listen to my words of recommendation, or would they blow me off as not knowing what I was talking about? I was deeply concerned that they might make poor choices, and that I wouldn't be able to save them from the impending consequences of their decisions.

When we approached the teenage years, my husband and I treated our children as we always had. We kept them busy. We had consistently had an active family life, and we didn't change that just because our kids became teenagers. In fact, we kept them more involved than ever.

During their younger years, we were continuously on the go. We didn't have a lot of money, but we found plenty to do. We took them hiking and bike riding. We would take them to ball games and the playground. The beach was a favorite place for the whole family. We went fishing frequently and, of course, there was the weekly trip to the ice cream stand during the summers. It wasn't a complete weekend without ice cream!

When the kids reached their teenage years, we found they still enjoyed doing these activities. So we kept doing them. And if they wanted to bring a friend or cousin along with them, we didn't mind. The more, the merrier.

And guess what – they flew through their teenage years with no trouble. Their early twenties were a little challenging because they struggled with trying to figure out where they wanted to live, what they wanted to do, and who they wanted to be with, but that's another story. They had successfully made it into adulthood, and had the rest of their lives to sort out the questions they now faced.

Maybe we were just lucky. Who's to say for sure. But don't back away from your kids during their teenage years or be afraid to spend time with them. Continue to keep them busy and occupied. And don't think you need to spend a lot of money doing it. An occasional trip to an amusement park is fun, but kids can find happiness in the simple things in life – like hiking, a family bike ride, picnics, camping and campfires, toasting marshmallows, roasting hot dogs........whatever it takes to keep them busy and, as a result, out of trouble.

MOMMA'S ROLE

Everyone has a role to play in family life. In our family, dad works to support the family, keeps the cars and yard in shape, and does the necessary maintenance around the house. Mom's role is to keep the family operating smoothly by making sure the laundry and dishes are done, maintaining the household chores, and keeping harmony in the home. And the children – well, they do what kids do. And that is where we sometimes run into trouble. When kids act like kids and get out of line, Momma's role takes on a whole different level of expertise.

I must admit that as hard as I try, sometimes the 'harmony' piece is just not within my grasp. So when things get noisy, crazy, or just plain out of control, what's a mother to do? Well, since it is usually the kids that are out of line, she can start by offering them a spot on the time-out bench. Or if things have escalated beyond the effect of the bench, then maybe an invitation to take a trip to their bedroom for a mini vacation is in order.

In our household, when harmony flies out the window, dad usually sails out the door. When the atmosphere inside the house is less than pleasant, my husband usually decides there is something outside that needs his immediate attention, like mowing the grass or raking the leaves.

It's great that he can escape the chaos, and possibly blow off some steam, but what can mom do to de-escalate? It's not like she can run away from the problems (also known as the kids.) So while dad is escaping to the great outdoors and the kids are on holiday in their bedrooms, mom is left to fend for herself.

Now as distressing as the loss of harmony in the household can be, it is important that mom pull it together. We've all heard the saying, "If Momma ain't happy, ain't nobody happy!" In our household, experience has proven this to be true! Moms can get upset, too, but no one can send Momma to her room if she is misbehaving, because she runs the household.

(And keeps it running smoothly, right?!)

But fortunately for mom, her role provides a lot of adequate ways to vent. For one thing, there is sweeping the floor. I have found sweeping to be a great way to vent my frustrations. But if sweeping doesn't do it for you, then you can always get down on your hands and knees to scrub the floor clean. And wow, stripping the bed down to change the sheets can really let some steam escape. Isn't it funny how Momma's household work can be so beneficial with venting her frustration?!

One thing about it, you can always tell when Momma isn't happy - because when Momma ain't happy, she sure can make the house shine! The poor floors probably hate it when the kids get her upset! So scrub away, Momma, until you've got it all out of your system. But don't forget your role. You are the restorer of the harmony in the home. Once the house is clean and shiny, round up those vacationers and pull your family back together. Hey, how about this? Maybe you could all go outside and help dad rake some leaves! I'm sure he would love the company!

NEVER A BURDEN

Working in a technical office, I am frequently asked questions that I do not have the answer for. When this happens, it is up to me to contact the appropriate person to get the necessary answer. Sometimes it is not urgent, and it can be dealt with through a return phone call. At other times, the answer needs to come a little quicker. With the office as busy as it is, that can sometimes be a challenge.

However, through years of experience, I have found there is always one employee that I can count on. She is one of the busiest people in the office, yet she is always willing to help. No matter what she is involved with, she will always stop and take the time to answer my question. She doesn't roll her eyes or act annoyed that I have interrupted her busy routine. She will simply pause long enough to make sure I have the information that I need.

Each time I walk away from her desk, I feel very thankful. I am grateful that she considered my question important enough to stop what she was doing to address it, and also pleased that I was able to get an answer to pass onto the person who is waiting. Plus, she never makes me feel like my question is stupid, even if I don't present the information properly or mispronounce something. That is not true with some of the other employees.

I no longer work in that office, but as I think back on it, I realize I learned a lot from her. I hope that I can be as helpful and patient with my children as she always was with me. I hope they can always feel as though their questions matter, and that what they are dealing with is not too trivial for me to stop what I am doing and help them out. When they mispronounce something or don't get their facts quite right, I hope I can gently correct them without making them feel self-conscious about their mistake. And most important of all, may I never make them feel like they are a burden to me.

ONLY RAIN

This morning when attempting to drop a child off at school, I got stuck in a traffic jam. It wasn't on the way to school, though. No, this was more like a bottle-neck jam in the school parking lot. The problem was that it was raining, and the parents all wanted the closest parking space, the one located directly in front of the school.

It seemed like some of the parents were willing to sit in the traffic jam all day and wait for that particular parking space, if that's what it took. I, on the other hand, had concerns about being late for work. But what could I do? There was no way to get around the traffic in front of me.

So while I sat there and stewed about it, I couldn't help but wonder why we work so hard to keep our kids sheltered. Why not just prepare them for the elements and let them deal with it? They are going to face many rainy days in their lifetime, so why shield them from them? I think the better plan would be to teach them how to deal with it instead.

Here is what I think parents should do on a rainy school day. Put boots and a raincoat on your child. When you get to the school, get out of the car to show them that rain does not hurt, nor does it make people melt. Open the car door, put their hood on, kiss them goodbye, and tell them to have a good day. Then sit in the car and watch them walk away. I'm sure you will find that it truly is only rain, and your child will somehow survive it!

POSITIVE DISCIPLINE

Parenting a four year old can be quite a challenge. They are old enough to get themselves into trouble, yet not experienced enough to keep themselves out of it. They haven't necessarily learned what is and is not considered acceptable behavior. And they seem to want to challenge everything to figure it out.

My son was no exception. He wanted to do things his way, and he was not interested in anything I had to say. It was his way, or the highway. Probably a typical, defiant, four-year old boy, actually.

Anyway, somewhere along the way, I had heard about a book on positive discipline. It was highly recommended, and I knew I could use all the help I could get. So I called the bookstore and ordered a copy of it.

A short time later, the bookstore called to let me know it had arrived. My husband and defiant child rode over with me to pick it up. They sat in the car while I quickly ran into the store to get it.

Apparently, at some point in time, our young son must have heard us discussing this book. I was very excited about it, and immediately took it out of the bag after getting situated in the car. Before I had really had a chance to look at it, though, I heard a little voice from the backseat pipe up.

"Let me see that book," he demanded.

I looked at my husband, who only shrugged, and then I handed the book back to him. He turned it over, as if he was reading the back cover. I couldn't help but smile, yet what he said next made me outright laugh.

"Oh, yeah," he said, pointing at the writing on the book, "It says right here that when the kid misbehaves, you hit him over the head with a frying pan!"

Man, where did this kid come from?! I have no idea where he came up with the idea, but I should have known right then that life was going to be an adventure with this one!

SCHOOL VACATION

My routine doesn't change much during the summer, since I still have to work all day, but that of my children does. This only adds to the complication of being a working mother. Now I have to worry about what kind of trouble my children are getting into while I am away for the day. They are old enough to no longer require a babysitter, but that doesn't mean they are capable of keeping themselves occupied and out of trouble – especially my daughter.

Today I went to work as usual, and my daughter called me about eight times throughout the day. She was bored and just couldn't figure out what to do with herself.

"Mom, can I go to Sarah's house?" to which I replied, "No, her mother isn't home."

The next call asked, "Mom, can I go swimming in the river with Amber?" and the reply was, "No, the current is too fast and you can't go to the river without an adult anyway."

It seemed every other phone call was my daughter, and the topic was always the same, "I'm bored!"

I had little to offer her. I was tied up at work and limited with entertainment ideas. I suggested she wash the dishes or do some laundry but, naturally, those were not on her list of fun things to do. The best I could offer was that she find something constructive to do with herself, and prayed she would follow my advice. However, when I got home, it was obvious she thought I had said to find something destructive, not constructive.

"I thought girls were supposed to be made of sugar and spice and everything nice," I muttered to myself, as I struggled to put her bureau drawer back together.

"I didn't do that!" she insisted.

"Sure," I mumbled to myself, "my bureau drawers always fall apart by themselves, too!"

Next, I went to the camper and tried to repair the table she had broken. She knew it was supposed to fold down somehow, and it appears that when all else failed, she sat on it! "Looks like this one is going to be a job for Dad," I grumbled to myself.

Then I went back into the house to try to put my kitchen back together. She had tried to make some cookies, but it wasn't clear whether those little briquettes sitting on the countertop were edible or not. And Heaven forbid that she clean up the kitchen when Mom would be home at any minute to do it for her!

So forget the 'sugar and spice and everything nice' girl. My daughter is more like a rock 'em, sock 'em robot! Hopefully school will start again soon. And I hope I have a house left by then!

STEAMING EARS

My son was a challenging child, there was no doubt about it. I often dreaded taking him into the store because he always wanted something, and he wasn't afraid to pitch a fit if he didn't get it. I was taking a course that taught how sometimes it is best to just ignore the undesirable behavior. Giving a lot of attention to bad behavior might only encourage it to continue.

One day at a store, he was once again having a meltdown because he couldn't get something he wanted. He was still preschool age, and I was taking care of a baby that day. Somehow I managed to get everyone out of the store, but that was as far as we made it. He folded his arms on the sidewalk and refused to take another step.

I had my hands full with trying to carry the baby and the bag of purchases, so I decided this was one of those times to ignore the bad behavior. I thought if I kept walking away, he would get concerned about being left behind and run to catch up with me. It seemed like a good plan, but it didn't work. I walked away as far as I dared, which wasn't far. However, looking over my shoulder, I could see that he hadn't budged.

He had tried my patience long enough. I turned around, marched back over to him, set the baby carrier and the bag down to free my hands. I took him by the shoulders and gave him a quick, serious, probably louder than I intended, face-to-face discussion. (Or was it more like nose-to-nose?!) I then instructed him to head for the car, and, fortunately, he cooperated.

However, I was now a mess. I had just made quite a scene with my child in public. I was worried about who might have seen it and if they would call the authorities because they felt I hadn't handled it properly. Plus, I was exhausted from the mental battle of it all, as well as the physical struggle of getting two young children and a bag of purchases successfully into the car.

I started to drive out of the parking lot, thinking there

was probably steam coming out of my ears. Why do kids have to do things like this? Why do they have to push your buttons in public and make such a scene? Why couldn't he have just cooperated and behaved himself? And why did I have to get so flustered and upset?

All these thoughts were floating around in my overheated brain when I heard this little voice in the backseat say, "What's for lunch, Mom?"

Seriously?! My ears were still steaming, my body overheating from the stress of the whole incident, wondering if there would be any repercussions from it, and he had already forgotten about it. He had moved on to lunch, as though none of what just happened mattered!

Kids! They say you've got to love them, and I do, but sometimes they push me to the limits, and sometimes even beyond!

SURROUNDED BY ENERGY

The energy was everywhere. I was outside in the yard, accompanied by my son and the dog. My son ran freely around the yard, pulling his blue, plastic sled behind him. It didn't seem to matter to him that the snow was gone. He was having a great time anyway.

The dog came running over and dropped a tennis ball at my feet. I bent down to pick it up and threw it across the yard. I watched in amazement as he sailed into the air to catch it. How could he do that?

Such energy running around my yard, and yet I was exhausted. Where had my energy gone? Then it hit me – I had given it to them. Getting up during the night to comfort my son when he had a nightmare. Getting up early in the morning to let the dog outside because he was whimpering to go. Feeding both of them routinely, keeping them clean and well cared for. I had been doting on their needs and giving them most of my time and attention, which ultimately resulted in giving them all of my energy, too.

The dog dropped the ball at my feet again. I picked it up, smiled and threw it across the yard. Yes, maybe I had given my energy away, but it was all worth the effort. It was time well invested. My son was healthy and happy, as was the dog running after the ball I just threw.

Maybe some day my energy will return when they are gone and I have time for myself. But I won't count on it. By then I will probably be too old to function properly and will be content to sit around in my rocking chair and knit!

THE BEAUTY OF COMMUNICATION

It is always a pleasure to have a legitimate reason to sleep in. I have never been one who enjoys jumping out of bed in the morning to start another day. There are times when it feels like I am up at least an hour before I finally wake up! I have often told my husband that I don't manage to fully open both eyes until I am halfway to work.

Today my daughter had an appointment at the beginning of the day, so it allowed me the opportunity to sleep in a little longer. I would go into work later than usual, after her appointment was over. It sounded like a perfect plan, but I apparently failed to communicate this information to all members of the family.

My normal routine is to get up at 6:00 each morning. Today I planned on sleeping in until at least 6:30, maybe even allowing myself the luxury of keeping the bed warm until 7:00. However, at quarter after six my son decided to let the dogs out, and then proceeded to stand beside my bedroom door and call to them. And then when they came back in, he decided to play with them beside my bedroom door, getting them into a frenzied state of barking. How could I sleep with all that racket going on?

Finally, I got up in frustration to address the situation. I told him it was too early in the morning to be playing so loudly with the dogs. He replied that he didn't want me to be late for work, but he hadn't dared to come wake me up. (Smart boy! He has learned through the years that I wake up a little on the grumpy side, and it is best not to disturb me if it can be avoided!)

So he thought he was doing a good deed by waking me up so I wouldn't be late for work, while I was upset with him for interrupting my opportunity to sleep in. The bottom line is that I need to learn to communicate a little better. My failure to adequately communicate with my family had just cost me the rare opportunity of an extra hour of sleep!

So you better believe the next time, I will make sure all

members of the family know when I plan on sleeping in – even if I have to hang a large, red-lettered Do Not Disturb sign on my bedroom door!

THE CLOCK MAKER

There are times (many times) when I wish life did not revolve around the clock. Some weeks it seems like I am trying to beat the clock from Monday morning straight through Friday night. I often wish I could tie the clock hands together so I would have more time to get things done (as if that would really work!)

For awhile, my husband and I tried building and selling mantel clocks. Although they were beautiful, we gave up when we failed to find a market for them. He now has them neatly arranged on a shelf where we can still enjoy their beauty. Only one of them is equipped with a battery, but the rest of them are right at least twice a day! (Sorry, that's an old joke!)

One night I was putting my daughter to bed and she was fighting me all the way. Bedtime has never been a favorite part of her day. She hates to close her eyes and go to sleep because she is afraid she will miss something. Plus it means she has to stop talking!

I tried to be patient, but she had pushed me beyond my level of tolerance. I finally stormed out of her room, leaving her with tears in her eyes, while I commented, "It's not my fault it's bedtime! I didn't make the clock!"

I stopped at the door of her bedroom, knowing this was not how I wanted to end our day, but yet not knowing if I had the energy to salvage what was left of it. That's when I heard this little, teary voice innocently say, "No, Daddy did!"

Well, I couldn't argue with her there. Daddy had made just about every clock in the house, even though most of them no longer worked. It's funny how kids can turn meanings around. They take things at face value. What I meant was that I couldn't control time, while she envisioned an actual clock! What does the Bible say – "out of the mouth of babes?!"

So here's a thought for you: As your clock of life ticks away, don't forget to enjoy every minute of it and love your kids. They grow up much faster than you may realize.

THE SPECIAL BOOK

My grandson had spent the night, and he had gotten up on the wrong side of the bed. No matter what I said or did, we just couldn't seem to get his behavior under control. It was like he had polished off a two liter bottle of soda and now had an abundance of energy. I tried all my usual approaches and behavior management techniques, but nothing seemed to be working. He just couldn't seem to pull it together.

Finally, after a long tiresome day of corrections, he took on an attitude of defeat. We were driving home from the beach and the little voice in the backseat said, "You don't like me anymore, Grandma. I'm just a stupid kid."

Just hearing him speak those words broke my heart. He was wrong. I loved him with all my heart, and he was far from a stupid kid. He was very clever, but the behavior piece was out-of-whack today. I knew I had to try to correct his thinking, so I said, "I love you, sweetie, and you are not a stupid kid. You are a very smart boy. But I think we need to take a break right now and not talk. So let's be quiet for the rest of the ride home."

For some reason, this piece of advice worked. Maybe he was just tired from playing at the beach. Whatever the reason, it gave us both a chance to think and regroup. As I drove home in silence, I thought about how much this child meant to me and wondered how I could make him understand how important he was.

Then I happened to remember the book I had made for him when he was little. I had printed pictures of some of the fun things we had done, and then had written captions to go along with each picture. It had taken me hours to put it together, but it had been worth the effort.

When we got home, I told him I had something to show him. I pulled out the book and went through some of the pictures with him. I explained that he was my grandson, so that made him a very special person to me. I would always love him, and he would always have a special place in my life. I told him that any time he gets discouraged and thinks nobody likes him or feels that he is just a 'stupid kid,' he should pull out this book and look at all the fun things we have done together. That would remind him of how special he is to me.

Just taking a few minutes to go through that book with him made a big difference. After that, he seemed to settle down and I didn't have any more trouble with him. It worked so well, I think I will make up a book for his younger brothers, too. That way, when they get older and start talking (and have a difficult day like we had today) I can show them their special book, too.

Everyone needs to know that they are special, and a Special Book for each child is a perfect idea! Plus, they are fun to make. It will remind me of all our fun times together while I work on it. This just might prove to be therapeutic for me, too!

THE THRILL OF POTTY TRAINING

Potty training was not one of my favorite stages in raising children. I'm not sure if I didn't have the patience, the proper techniques, or if I just plain stunk at it. Whatever the reason, I felt like a failure from the beginning to the end of the nasty, little task.

It's not that I didn't try all the suggested techniques. Since I was training a boy, someone had told me to put targets in the toilet that he could pee on. So I threw cereal in the toilet bowl so he could do some target practice. Another person told me to let him pee in a bottle. She said boys thought that was really cool.

I tried it all, and didn't have much trouble with the peeing part of the training. It was what came out the other end that was a problem. He just didn't want to be bothered with taking time from his play to do his bowel movements. And nothing I said seemed to make a difference.

Finally, I decided we were just going to use underwear. If he didn't use the toilet, he would soil his pants. And so he did! Over and over again, we ended up with soiled underwear. It became tedious and very tiresome rinsing out his dirty pants. So I decided if he was going to soil his underwear, then he could deal with them.

I shared my plan with him, telling him if he didn't use the potty the right way and made a mess of his underwear, he would have to rinse them out himself. Surprisingly, he was agreeable with this plan. I thought I had come up with the perfect solution. After rinsing out a few pair of dirty underwear, he might decide it was easier to use the potty.

The next time he soiled his underwear, I reminded him of our agreement. I expected an argument, but he was agreeable to washing his dirty undergarments. So I got a stool for him to stand on, filled the bathroom sink with water and laundry soap, and told him to go to work. Then I sat back and gloated. This would surely teach him the value of properly using the toilet.

We all know how kids can turn the tables and ruin the best of plans we make as parents. Imagine my surprise when I heard him singing in the bathroom while he was washing his dirty underwear! I poked my head in the doorway, thinking he was probably playing instead of washing, but he wasn't. There he stood, as sweet as any child could be, diligently washing his soiled underpants while singing his favorite childhood song! Man, did I feel defeated!

We were finally successful with the potty training, but I said the next child we had was going to come fully potty trained or I wasn't playing the game!!

TUBBY TIME

As a method of saving time, we frequently give the boys a bath together. It is so much quicker and easier to just do it as a unit. And they like playing together in the tub, so what harm could there be in letting them bathe together? They enjoy sharing bath toys and washing each other's hair. Not only does it get them clean, but it's one of the rare times when they aren't fighting.

Last night while bathing them, one of the boys was acting a little unusual. Instead of sitting in the tub, he was sort of hovering over the water in a squatting position. I didn't think much about it. I just figured he was working his way into the water slowly. But all of a sudden, he started freaking out. He was pointing at the water and yelling in his toddler babble, which makes absolutely no sense to anyone but him and his brother.

It turns out that he was squatting because he had to poop. It's not something that hasn't happened in the bathtub before. We have had little logs floating in the tub in the past, but this time he was not happy about it.

He stood up and started screaming while he pointed at it floating around in the bath water. Things really got funny when he tried to get away from it. He climbed over into the corner to hide behind his brother, looking at the bowel movement like it was an alligator trying to bite him!

It was actually kind of comical. He seemed terrified of it, as if he had never seen poop before. It was like he couldn't figure out what it was or where it had come from.

That's when things got funny. The log didn't seem to bother his brother at all. He just looked at it casually, then picked it up and handed it to me.

It was like he was saying, "Uh, there's something in the tub that doesn't belong here!"

Now there are a lot of things I wouldn't mind someone handing to me – like a box of chocolates, or a large check with my name on it. But I have to say that a handful of poop ranks pretty close to the bottom of the list, if not on the bottom! Oh, the joys of being a mother. You just never know what will come your way next!

WINDOW OF OPPORTUNITY

Nice – the kids were asleep and I finally had some time for myself. It wasn't often that they took a nap at the same time, and after such a busy morning, I was thankful for the break. Now I would have some uninterrupted time to actually accomplish some housework.

I looked at the pile of dirty dishes and decided that was my next task. After that, I would tackle the mountain of dirty clothes in the laundry room. However, first I was going to take a few minutes for myself. I would enjoy a cup of hot tea and take a breather before taking on the household chores. After a busy morning of kid care, I deserved some time to myself.

As I settled down at the table with my cup of tea, the telephone rang. It was my sister calling. We hadn't talked for quite awhile, so it turned out to be a lengthy conversation. When the call finally ended, I hung up the phone, took the final sip of my tea, and headed toward the sink to take on the dirty dishes.

After cleaning the sink out, I organized what needed to be washed, rolled up my sleeves and prepared to start washing. I ran some clean water, poured some dish soap into the sink, and hummed peacefully to myself. Then I carelessly dropped a handful of silverware into the sink.

Who knows if it was the clanging on the silverware as it hit the stainless steel sink, or if it was just the hand of fate, but the baby started crying. I groaned and realized I had missed my window of opportunity. If you are a mother, you know what I mean. I'm talking about that narrow little window of opportunity that would have allowed me to get some housework done without any interruptions!

Oh, well – some day the kids will grow up and I will have ample opportunities to do housework without interruptions. Next time, maybe I will work harder to use my window of opportunity wisely. Not that talking to my sister hadn't been beneficial. It's just that my household chores were still not done, and now I had to focus on kid duty again.

So here's the plan for next time: either I will talk faster, put my phone on speaker so I can work while I talk, or maybe put the silverware in the sink a little more quietly!

YOUR GREATEST INVESTMENT

Sometimes children seem to be angry, or sometimes determined to prove themselves right and everyone else wrong. Sometimes it seems they just want to argue, or be sassy and rude. And there are times when respecting their elders just doesn't seem to be a priority for them.

Back a generation or so, families didn't have a lot of money, but they did have time for each other. A family picnic was a special event. Kids were content to simply go to the beach or the local community park. In today's society, a family event is more likely to be a trip to a costly amusement park, where it's easy to lose lots of money. And then, in the meantime, we shower them with gifts at home – things like game systems, name brand clothing and shoes – and then work all the time to pay for what we probably charged on our credit cards.

What if we went back to the days of spending more time with our kids, and less money on them? It's not the money and gifts that will shape them into something we can be proud of. I believe, instead, that it is the quality time we invest in them that makes the difference. They need to know who they are, that they belong somewhere and to someone. They need to know that they are a part of a family, and that it is important enough for us to take time out of our busy schedule to spend time with them. The bottom line is that they need to feel loved.

So shut off the television, take those violent video games away, tuck your wallet back into your pocket, and get the fishing poles out. Lace up your sneakers and go for a hike. Get your bikes out, oil the chains, and take a ride together. Or pack a picnic lunch and take a walk to the park. Invest some time into your children, and perhaps they will relax and let go of their anger once they develop a sense of belonging and realize how important they are to you. Nothing shows them love and how much they mean to you more than spending time with them. And don't worry about the housework and dirty laundry. It will still be there when you get home! (I have years of experience to support that statement!) Your children will grow up and be gone some day, and then you will have plenty of time for your dirty house!

So remember that your children are the greatest investment you will ever make. It's a life time investment, with many happy returns. So be sure to make a memorable deposit into your account each day, not a monetary one!

ENDING THOUGHTS ON THE JOYS OF PARENTING

Before I became a parent, I had no idea how much work it would be. I had been around kids all my life. Not only had I come from a large family, but my mother provided child care for many, many children in town. I followed in her footsteps and started providing child care services myself at a young age. But when I became a parent, having children around 24/7, and not being able to return them to their rightful owner at the end of my shift, I discovered it was more work than I had anticipated.

It's not that I didn't love my children. Oh, I loved them all right – when they weren't driving me nuts! I was actively involved in their childhood and trying to raise them properly, but the role of motherhood was exhausting. Since I was a stay-at-home mother, I never got a break from their constant needs.

Yet, at the same time, I knew how truly blessed I was. To help get me through the challenging, needy years of my children's lives, I started keeping a journal of the cute, little things they said and did. I knew they were too precious to let them slip away without recording them in some manner. Even now as adults, I have certain text messages they have sent to me that I just cannot delete. They are memories that are worth reviewing, reliving, and finding humor in repeatedly.

Since my children have all grown and moved into their own homes, I can tell you that you can survive the needy years. My advice would be to not sweat the little things. Don't let the constant demands drive you crazy. And if it is helpful to you, keep a journal of all the sweet moments that will someday make awesome memories. Jot them down somewhere so it will become a recorded memory you can relive over and over, just like looking at old photos.

And on those days when you are at wits end and pulling your hair out, be strong and know that all good things come to an end, and so will the years of being an active parent. Let's face it – if we knew in advance how challenging parenthood could be, there would probably be fewer parents in the world. But then life would cease to exist – literally!

It helps to know that your children will provide you with some of the happiest memories you will ever have, and just might become your best friends in adulthood. Plus they are the ones who provide you with grandchildren, and being a grandmother is a role I wouldn't trade for the world!

So hang in there, parents! Realize how precious your little ones are, and know that what you do in your life can change the course of theirs. And always remember that you will never hold a more important position in life. You can do it, Mom and Dad!!

For the Spirit

For the Spirit

ABOUT FOR THE SPIRIT

Often times we get so busy in life that we overlook and neglect the spiritual being which exists in each of us. However, it is as important to feed, nurture, and exercise this spiritual side as it is our physical body. If we don't give this needed and vital attention to our internal self, it will become weak and wither away.

As with previous articles, the writings in For the Spirit are random views and reflections that I recorded at different stages in my life. Some of them have a humorous tone to them, while others are more personal and intense. These are thoughts that I jotted down as God spoke to my soul. It seemed if it was important enough for Him to share these concepts with me, they were significant enough to pass on to others that might benefit from them, too.

God continues to be alive and well, and He is interested in us as individuals. He cares about the challenges we face, the life we are living, and the choices we make. While it would be helpful for Him to shout His will from the mountaintop or send daily broadcasts telling us what He wants us to do, He is more apt to speak in a still, small voice. His messages are more subtle, and can become clear to those who take the time to seek and search for the answers they need.

I hope you find the articles in *For the Spirit* to be refreshing and reassuring to your soul. Sometimes, even after reading them numerous times, they can still bring tears to my eyes and touch my very soul. I pray that these stories will bless you as well.

A LUKEWARM LESSON

There is a verse in the Bible that I have always had trouble understanding. It is Revelation 3:16, where God says that if we are lukewarm, He will spit us out.

To be honest, that verse has always baffled me. If He were to reject anyone, I would think it would be someone who is cold. To be cold is usually associated with being hard-hearted or uncaring. At least if you were lukewarm, you wouldn't be cold. Yet it is the lukewarm people He would refuse. It made me wonder what is wrong with being lukewarm.

One day it was like a light bulb came on. A person who is hot is typically seeking a way to regulate the heat. Maybe it is through fanning yourself to get cool. Perhaps one might be looking to purchase an air conditioner, or digging in a closet for a box fan. Whatever the case, you won't be satisfied with staying uncomfortably warm.

On the flip side of that is the state of being too cold. When one is cold, they are actively seeking a blanket to wrap up in, or looking for extra clothing to put on. Sitting still and silently freezing to death is not an option. As with being too hot, you will be seeking a change.

However, when we are lukewarm, we are satisfied with our state of comfort. We are not actively seeking anything. In a lukewarm state, we are not too hot, nor are we too cold. We are just right, and when one is comfortable and content, they quite frequently fall asleep. (Like I do while wrapped up in a blanket and sitting on the couch watching television!)

That verse finally makes sense to me! God doesn't want us to be comfortable Christians who are content with our current state. He wants us to remain in a constant state of activity, pursuing Him and continuously seeking our calling in life. To be lukewarm means we could find ourselves asleep in a state of comfort, and fall short of the quality of life that only He can provide. May we always be seeking Him and His will for our lives, and never become content with snoozing comfortably on the couch while life passes us by!

A REFRESHING SILENCE

The song service at church was awesome. Our church has been blessed with a lot of young talent. The youth are alive as they share their love for God through their musical abilities. The guitars, keyboard, and drums resonate with worship to God every Sunday morning.

I absolutely love to sing along and bellow out the melodies of praise. God has blessed me with a nice singing voice. It was a talent I did not acquire from my mother, though. She couldn't carry a tune in a bucket. (Those were her words, not mine!)

Today was different, though. I just didn't feel like singing, which was totally unusual for my character. For some reason, today I wanted to sit silently and simply rest. My soul seemed to whisper:

"Don't speak. Don't say a word.
Don't ask for anything or even think.
Just sit back, bask in His love, and
soak up the presence of the Lord.
Just like Mary in the Bible,
you don't need to say or do anything
to feel the refreshing presence of His love."

And so I did. I just basked in His presence, and it was as refreshing as a day at the beach, soaking up the sun, or listening to the sounds of life - like the cool water splashing peacefully on the shoreline. It was as refreshing as drawing in a deep breath and reveling in simply being alive, just enjoying the feeling of existence.

The silent times can be a great time of spiritual renewal. It doesn't always take words to feel His presence and know how much He cares about us. Sometimes we just need to sit silently at His feet and allow Him to saturate us with peace and love. How refreshing a time of silence can be!

A SORE THROAT BLESSING

I woke up with a sore throat again. It has been happening for about a week now. It's possible I need to keep my mouth closed while I sleep, or maybe it's due to the dry air since it is winter time and the heating system is on.

Anyway, when I woke up, my first thought was to be upset. I thought "This is not fair! I am so tired of waking up every morning with a sore throat. When is this ever going to end?!"

I often wake up a little on the grumpy side anyway. Early morning is not my favorite part of the day. I just don't like to get up and leave the comfort of my bed. So as I lay there and contemplated my sore throat, while feeling upset about it, I began to feel the desire to laugh.

Who was I to complain about something so silly? There are a lot of people in the world that would rejoice at having such a trivial problem. I thought of my husband, who has to moan and groan his way out of bed every morning because his back hurts so badly. Then there are the elderly whose bodies are so worn out they might not even be able to get out of bed at all, without some type of assistance. And what about the people who have some form of paralysis and can't walk? Or the ones who suffer from severe pain related to cancer or some other serious illness?

And you're complaining about a sore throat, Kitty?! It's nothing you are going to die from. You don't need to run to the doctor and get an antibiotic. It won't keep you from doing what you need to do today. It's not a life-threatening condition. I think you just might survive this!

My thought process changed and instead of starting my day by griping, I started thanking God that my only complaint was a simple sore throat. It is great to count our blessings, because we often have a lot more to be thankful for than we realize. And the fact that my greatest complaint of the morning was having a sore throat was truly something to rejoice about!

A SPIRITUAL WORKOUT

Walking by the gym, I glanced in and saw an elderly gentleman working out at one of the machines. It almost put me to shame, watching his effort and knowing that I would benefit from something similar. He was doing all he could to strengthen his muscles and keep his body in shape. I'm sure he was more fit than me, even though he was obviously much older.

As I walked away, my thought process took a turn. What about my spiritual side? That needs a routine workout, too. Was I doing all I could to keep my spiritual man in shape? Was I working diligently to keep my heart and mind in tune with God?

I thought back to a religious concert my husband and I had attended recently, and I can honestly say that was a spiritual workout! I was totally exhausted when we left. Throughout the concert, I sang, and danced, and shouted praises to God. The rapture could haven taken place during the concert, and I would not have even noticed. I was so caught up in God's glory, I probably wouldn't have noticed if I had floated away!

But concerts like that are few and far between, and your spirit needs a workout more frequently. So it is important for us, on a daily basis, to remain focused on God. Flood yourself with Christian music, Bible reading, prayer time, and don't forget to take advantage of the programming offered on the Christian television networks. I find I don't have a lot of free time, so I watch Christian programming on television while getting ready for work. Then I listen to a Christian radio station while driving. Sometimes what I hear speaks directly to my soul. It couldn't be more personal than if God had spoken to me Himself!

So take time for yourself, and make sure you keep your body in shape - and not just the physical piece. Take time for the spiritual side as well. And just like that old man at the gym, don't ever give up because you think you are past the point of needing a workout. Our spiritual man (or woman!) needs to stay in shape, too, right to the very end! You are never too old to learn something new or need a daily workout!

A SWEET REPLY

It wasn't fair. I was trying to cover my coworker's position so she could take a much needed vacation, and things were not going well. There was one particular person who seemed determined to ruin my day. I was doing all I could to try to help her, but apparently it wasn't enough. And then she called and left me an unfriendly message. She didn't swear at me, but she made it clear that I wasn't meeting her need, even though I felt I was doing all I could to try to help her.

In a situation like this, the natural reaction is to get upset or angry. That old flesh wants to put other people in their place. This person had not clearly explained what she needed, so it wasn't fair that she be upset with me for not understanding. And I felt like calling her back and telling her just that. I wanted to let her know that I don't read minds. How could she expect me to know what she needed if she didn't tell me?

However, I knew that wasn't the right solution. The Bible tells us that we are to forgive and forget. It also teaches us to resolve issues quickly before they have the chance to get bigger. So I didn't take the time to sit there and fume about it. I picked up the telephone and called her back to see how I could help. She didn't answer, so I left a soft, sweet message telling her that I was sorry I had misunderstood her, and also that I would make sure everything was taken care of as soon as possible. And I left it at that for the day.

The next morning, I checked my coworker's messages and groaned when I heard the same voice on her voicemail. However, this time she had called to apologize for her attitude and thanked me for the help.

Wow – what a difference a sweet reply can make. Had I left a rude message for her, she would have called back and left another for me. And on and on it could have gone. But the sweet reply stopped the bitterness in its tracks! The Bible does know what it's talking about. I had put it to the test, and guess what – it worked!!!

ANGEL EYES

Arriving at work, I noticed there was a little, gray cat walking across the parking lot. I had never seen this cat before, and I immediately noticed how thin it was. Not just skinny, really. This cat looked sick.

It caught me off guard when the cat walked right toward me. Of course, I was friendly and said hello as it approached. He (or she) walked right up to me, and I paused to give it a friendly pat. Then, feeling I had adequately displayed some compassion, I continued on my way.

Looking back, I noticed that the cat was acting odd. It had stopped right where we had met, and it was almost walking around in circles. It was like the cat had expected something more from me, and now it was lost and confused because he didn't get what he wanted.

Realizing he was probably starving, I glanced into my lunch bag to see if I had anything I might be able to offer him. There was a bag of croutons in there, so I took it out, held it up, and asked, "Are you hungry?"

The cat immediately came running toward me. I didn't want to feed him in the middle of the parking lot, for fear he might get run over, so I brought him to the edge of the lot and dropped a pile of croutons on the ground. It was stunning how quickly he started devouring them. The poor, little thing was starving.

Reaching into my bag again, I grabbed another handful and dropped it on the ground beside him. Then, not wanting to be late for work, I continued on my way across the parking lot. As I got to the door, I looked back to see if he was still eating. He was, but he paused long enough to look over his shoulder at me.

Maybe I read more into it than was actually there, but it appeared to be an amazing look. It was like he was thanking me for reaching out to help him. It kind of looked like angel's eyes staring back at me.

The experience made me think that if this was an angel

and I was being tested, just as a means of checking my level of compassion, I think I had just passed with flying colors. And if it was nothing more than a hungry, starving little cat, then I still scored well – in his eyes, anyway!

BEATEN AND BRUISED

It hadn't been just a rough day, it had been a long, difficult week. It seemed like I had done nothing but put out fires and solve problems for longer than I wanted to think about. Today had been especially challenging, so I decided to go to bed early.

My daily routine always includes reading my Bible before going to bed. Even though I was exhausted, both physically and emotionally, I knew it was important to not skip that portion of my day. So I opened my Bible to where I had left off the day before and started reading about Paul. It happened to be the chapter where the angry Jews dragged him out of the city and stoned him.

Wow – I could almost relate to that. I have never been physically abused, but it seemed like an adequate comparison to how I felt emotionally. Every time I turned around lately, it was like someone else was throwing another stone at me. And like Paul, I hadn't done anything wrong!

I set my Bible down and decided to have a heart-to-heart talk with God. I told Him all about my struggles and woes, as if He didn't already know. Then I closed my eyes and waited for His reply. And you know what, He reached out to me.

I felt His reassurance that what I was doing was right. Not all the challenges I had been dealing with were directly mine. Some of them pertained to a young family who didn't have the ability to advocate for themselves. I had taken on some of their struggles, trying to be a mediator for them, even though it was wearing me out.

However, as I lay there in my bed, I felt such a measure of peace from God. I felt like He was telling me what a good thing I was doing to reach out and help them. The outcome of their situations would probably be different if I wasn't there to lend a hand.

Then I pictured Paul, lying on the ground after they had stoned him. Did he stay there and give up in a heap of defeat? Did he decide to just quit and die where they had left him? No way – he got up and walked away. I pictured myself doing the same thing – rising up and stepping away from my problems, leaving them piled up just like the stones Paul had brushed off and left behind.

Just envisioning it gave me such joy and relief, I actually felt like giggling. I knew if I uttered a sound, the laughter would come, and I might not be able to stop it. So I kept the joy inside. My husband probably would have thought I had gone crazy if he heard me giggling in the bedroom by myself!

Will there be more challenges tomorrow? With the way things have been going, I imagine there probably will be. But with God's help, I will rise up and walk away from them. I may sometimes feel beaten and bruised, but knowing that God is with me, I never need to feel defeated.

FOCUS ON THE LIGHT

A heavy snow storm was in the forecast, but there was nothing I could do about it. At other times, I would have canceled my plans and stayed at home. But my daughter's surgery had been planned for months, and it wasn't something we should put off any longer. It needed to be taken care of.

I knew we could get to the hospital with no trouble, but the storm was due to start shortly after that. She would be spending the night, but it sounded like I would be making my way home in the thick of the storm.

As predicted, the snowfall started shortly after we arrived at the hospital. While she was in surgery, I sat in the waiting room watching the flurry of snowflakes falling to the ground. It was coming down intensely, like its mission was to bury the world in a sea of white, and it was doing a mighty fine job of it.

The maintenance crew kept me entertained. Instead of worrying about my daughter, I sat in the window and watched them shoveling sidewalks and plowing with the massive equipment it took to clear such a large parking lot. But all the while, I was thinking about driving home in the white blanket of fluff that was piling up deeper and deeper all the time. It may have looked beautiful from my vantage point in the warm waiting room looking out, but being outside in the midst of it would be a different story.

The surgery went fine, and the staff settled my daughter into her room. Not wanting to be out after dark, I told her I was going to clean my car off and get ready to go home. However, it took longer than I expected, and a short time later, I found myself driving home not just in the snow storm, but also in the darkness that had started to fall. Visibility from the storm was poor to begin with, but having darkness coming on only added to the difficulties. And this was some of the worse winter driving I had ever seen.

There were stretches of my drive home that were narrow and hard to negotiate on a good day, but this was far from a good day. I began to wonder if I would be able to even find my way home. But then God did something wonderful. He sent a truck to guide me.

Not far from the hospital, I came upon a truck which was apparently going in the same direction that I was. For over thirty minutes, I focused on the red taillights in front of me. As long as I could see them, it meant we were still on the road and moving forward. I didn't need to try to figure out where the road was. I just needed to keep my eyes on those lights. And they led me right to where I wanted to be – home!

Life is full of storms, some more intense than others. And I believe God does send us a light to guide us through the storms. As long as we focus on His guiding light instead of the intensity of the storm surrounding us, we can find our way home, no matter how difficult the traveling may be.

FROM THE MOUTH OF BABES

My eight-year old daughter had decided to bring a friend to the weekly after school youth group meeting. Her friend did not attend church regularly, but she had heard about the group and thought it sounded like fun.

The club leader was an interactive one. She liked to keep the kids involved by asking questions. They were eager to answer, and it held their interest. I agreed with her teaching style, and as club assistant, I settled down to aid in whatever way I could.

This week's lesson was about the life of Jesus. She was telling the children about the three years Jesus had lived on earth. She told them of His love for the children and how He had always taken time for them. She asked what they would have thought if they saw Jesus walking down the street, and then took the time to listen and build on their answers.

I watched my daughter's friend, and she remained wide-eyed and invested throughout the entire session. I'm not sure if the teacher knew that this little girl did not attend church, but she probably thought the question she was about to ask was a safe one for anyone to answer.

Turning to look at my daughter's friend, she said, "Now I have a question for you. Did Jesus ever sin?"

I watched as her face acquired a baffled look and she put her finger to her mouth. All she replied was, "Hmm...."

Realizing she may not know what the word 'sin' meant, I tried to help out. "Did Jesus ever do anything wrong?" I simplified for her.

"Oh," she said, looking like the light bulb had just come on. She nodded her head emphatically and answered, "Yeah, He did."

My face must have taken on a surprised look because she quickly added, "But only once!"

It was a nice attempt at a recovery, but it sounds like it might be beneficial for this little girl to attend a few more meetings!

GIVE AND TAKE

I have always thought life was supposed to be a game of give and take. You give what you can and then appreciate the gifts and blessings that come back to you. But sometimes it seems as though life is more of a game of 'Give, and Then Give Some More.' Maybe that's the role a mother plays, though.

I give all I've got to meet my family's needs. I work all day long, come home to make supper, wash the dishes, and then throw in a load of laundry. By the time I am done with the housework, I am exhausted and it's time to start the bedtime routine. I am rarely afforded the opportunity to sit down with the family and watch a television show. And do I get even a simple "Thank you" for all I do?

Are you kidding me? I get comments from my kids like, "Where are my favorite pair of jeans? I thought you said you did the laundry!" or "Spaghetti again? Didn't we just have spaghetti?!"

It just seemed to me like the scales were tipped a little too far to one side. I was doing all the giving while they were doing all the taking. And there was no point in trying to reason with them or bring this to their attention. They either didn't want to hear it, or didn't care anyway. They were still in the "All about me" stage of life.

A few days later, I was at church enjoying the song service. As I was singing my heart out to God, the whole 'Give and Take' scenario entered my mind. I felt like He was speaking to me about it, addressing this concern that was heavy on my heart.

He said, "I give continuously, too. I give you joy in a time of sorrow. I give peace in the midst of the storm. I give you strength when you are weak.

"And what do I take? I take the burdens that are too heavy for you to bear. I take away your discouragement, your distress, your despair. But above all, I take away your sins. And why do I do this? Because I love you."

Whoa – shame on me for my feelings of self pity. Not only does Jesus give above and beyond anything that I could ever ask, but He also takes away the stress of all that I cannot handle. And He does it all for the sake of love.

As I walk this road of life, may I be more like Jesus. By His example, I can learn to give what good, decent, positive things that I can without expecting some type of gift in return. I just need to remember all He does for me, and pass that kind of love on to my children, who may someday pass it on to children of their own!

GOOD THINGS COME...

My sisters and I wanted to go to the Statue of Liberty for a day trip, but we were having a hard time coordinating a day off. With the four of us all holding full-time positions, we just couldn't seem to find a day that would work for everyone. And each time we thought we had come up with one, something would happen to alter our plans.

It took all summer long, with multiple attempts, before we finally settled on a day in late August. It was the end of the summer, but the weather would still be warm. And on a positive note, school would back in session, so maybe it wouldn't be quite as busy.

However, when the day we had chosen finally arrived, I found myself unexpectedly at the hospital with a very ill loved one. I encouraged my sisters to take the trip without me, but they said it was a package deal. Either we all went, or no one did. I appreciated how special that made me feel, particularly in light of my situation. However, I still felt bad, knowing that I was the one who had kept our day trip from happening.

With the changing of the seasons, we had missed our opportunity to go to see the Statue. We decided the next year we would start early and choose a day before the summer got away from us. Yet, once again, we ran into numerous complications and found the summer fading away with no trip to the Statue of Liberty. This time, it was September before we could come up with a day that would work.

As the day grew closer, we discovered the Pope would be in New York City on the very day we had planned our trip. Did we really want to take on a trip to the Statue of Liberty on the same day as a visit from the Pope? The city was destined to be crazy with activity.

We talked about a different destination, but one sister was adamant. We had been trying to make this happen for two years now, so she felt we should stick to the plan. But before heading out, we put our heads together and came up with a backup plan. We decided we would leave from the

New Jersey side, and thus avoid the city altogether. And if the Statue proved to be too busy, we would visit Staten Island instead.

So off we went, and it looked like the weather was going to be perfect. The Statue was busy, but not overwhelmingly so. We took a trip over to Ellis Island and since it was lunch time, we grabbed a bite to eat and sat outside.

As I looked around, I felt so blessed. God had given me such wonderful sisters, and He had blessed us with perfect weather. Maybe He had provided us with such a beautiful day because He knew how long we had worked to get there. And I was glad one of my sisters had insisted on sticking with the original plan. We could now say we had finally reached our destination, and we couldn't have asked for a better day. God had truly been good to us.

Remember the saying, "Good things come to those who wait?" Well, we found out it is true – even if it does take two years to coordinate a simple day trip!

HE CARES

A couple of years ago, my whole family went on a vacation together. Both of our children had graduated from school, and my daughter was married with a family of her own. But we hadn't been on a vacation together for awhile, so we decided it was time. I booked a couple of cabins for us, and we headed to the seacoast with high hopes.

However, things don't always go according to our plans, as we all know. My son, his girlfriend, my husband and I would be staying in one cabin, while my daughter, her husband and young son would have a cabin of their own. When we arrived at our destination, I was disappointed to see how small the cabins were. I knew it would be tight quarters for the week, but decided we would make the best of it.

We were not far into the week, though, when things began to fall apart. The cabin was just not big enough for all of us. The table was too small for everyone to sit at, and we kept tripping over each other in the living room. My daughter spent most of her time at our cabin, and my husband and son quickly got tired of the baby crying and getting into everything. Things were just not going as well as I had hoped.

Then one night after supper, the bottom dropped out. I'm not really sure what triggered it all. It probably wasn't anything serious. I think it had something to do with the baby, because I said I had had enough and took him with me when I left. Now here is when something spectacular happened.

I headed down to the beach with the baby, and I saw the most amazing rainbow I have ever seen in my entire life. It was a double rainbow that stretched completely across the cove. But what was so amazing was that its origin started right at the head of the cove, directly off the point of the land.

As upset as I was about the family friction in my cabin, I turned around and ran to grab my camera. I think maybe God sent the rainbow to distract me from my problems, but I didn't get it. I just couldn't seem to let it go.

After I took about a dozen pictures of the double rainbow, I went back to the cabin to pout. I told everyone they could do what they wanted. I was heading to bed since this vacation wasn't going the way I wanted it to. And so I did.

I may have gone to bed, but I didn't go to sleep for a very long time. Instead I had a heart-to-heart talk with God. I had wanted a harmonious family vacation where we would make lots of wonderful memories, and here we were fighting with each other. I told God I needed some reassurance from Him, and asked Him to speak to me. Just give me some kind of a sign that He cared about me and what I was going through.

After what seemed like a very long time, I finally fell asleep. I was hoping to wake up refreshed, after having had a wonderful dream from God letting me know that He was there and was concerned about all of this. However, in the morning, I woke up still feeling beat up. I wasn't rejuvenated, nor had anything special happened during the night.

My first thought was that God didn't really care about me at all. But I have always had a hard time waking up in the morning, and knew I was just disappointed. I had really hoped for a special dream or some kind of sign from Heaven, yet nothing had happened. I couldn't even remember having had a dream at all.

I finally decided to get up and start over again. I realized it was up to me to set the tone for the rest of this vacation. If I wasn't happy, I would ruin the rest of the trip. (Remember - "If Momma ain't happy, ain't no one happy"?) So I determined to smile and be happy, and the rest of the week went wonderful. And we did make many happy, family memories.

As the week ended, we packed up our belongings and headed home. There was an old fort we wanted to stop and see along the way, so we pointed our cars in that direction. The fort was just as amazing as we had expected, and we had a great time.

Before leaving the fort, we checked the map to determine how we would head home. My husband and I chose a route that seemed to be the most practical one. Our son was following us with his car, so off we headed.

We hadn't gone far when we realized the car was making an unusual noise. And the further we drove, the louder the noise got. My husband is a mechanic, so he had noticed the noise, too. I asked him what he thought it was and what could happen if it didn't get fixed. He said it was possible that the axle could come apart, and we were traveling 50 mph down the road.

I kept hoping we would come across a garage where we could stop and ask someone about it, but the route we had chosen was very rural. We didn't even pass through any towns or villages. I could tell my husband was getting very concerned about the noise, but there wasn't much we could do except to keep driving.

As we drove, I saw a church with a billboard sign out front. I thought maybe there would be an encouraging message on the board. I was still hoping deep inside that God would give me a sign that he cared. However, this sign was not one of encouragement. It read, "Don't wait for a hearse to bring you to church." Yikes – that is not what I needed to see right now! A little further down the road, we saw a hearse sitting at the hardware store. All I could think was, "God, this is not really funny. I'm a little nervous right now."

All the time we were driving, I was praying. I asked God to help us find someplace that could fix our car quickly, so that we wouldn't be terribly inconvenienced, and also affordably, because I would have to charge it on my credit card. I kept thinking that if we found a garage that had to order parts, we would all have to find another place to stay for an extra night (or until they could get the part.) It had the potential to turn into a very costly repair job.

Finally, at an intersection, we saw a sign that pointed to a business district. I told my husband to turn. If they had a business district, then maybe they would have a garage that could help us. So we turned and came across a McDonald's. My husband decided to stop there so he could converse with our son and see what he thought about the problem.

We pulled into the McDonald's and got out of the car. My husband took our son for a ride so he could hear the noise, and the rest of us waited in the parking lot. As we waited, I saw a UPS truck parked close by. I decided that if anyone knew the area and where we might be able to find a garage that could help, a UPS man would. So I walked over to his truck, told him about our situation, and asked if he knew of any garages in the area. He said there was a Chevrolet car dealership just up the road, and he thought they did repair work there.

Well, that sounded about perfect to me. Our car was a Chevrolet, so they might be able to help us out. I would never have thought of going to a dealership for repair work, though. Yet we decided to give it a try.

When my husband and son came back, we headed up to the car dealership. There was actually a bay labeled Repairs, so we pulled in and told them what our problem was. They said they could help us, and had a mechanic on hand ready to do the job. We decided to go to McDonald's for lunch, and got the stroller out of the car to walk over. The mechanic was readily available, and actually had to wait for us to vacate the car so he could take it to the garage for the repair work!

We walked down to McDonald's, had some lunch, and then headed back to check on the car. As we walked into the parking lot, the mechanic drove over with our car. We expected him to say that there were more complications than he had expected, or that he had to order more parts before he could do anything. However, he had already finished the work and was driving the car over to bring it to us. He had fixed it while we were eating! And when I went in to pay the bill, I was surprised at how inexpensive the repair work had been.

We thanked them for helping us, and hopped back onto the highway to head home. As we drove down the road, I thought about everything that had just happened. If we hadn't gone to the fort, and if we hadn't chosen that particular route, and if we hadn't turned at the Business District sign, and if we hadn't stopped at McDonald's, and if I hadn't asked the UPS man, we never would have found a place that had the parts we needed on hand, and could repair the car quickly and inexpensively while we ate lunch. It had all been so beautifully orchestrated. I knew it couldn't have just happened by itself.

As I pondered it all, God spoke to my heart and said, "Don't ever think that I don't care about you." And just for one more measure of reassurance, when I got home and checked the mail, there was a card addressed to me. On the front cover of the card it said, "God cares about you." I opened it up and on the inside, it said, "Today I thought I would join Him." And it was signed by a secret sister.

I never did find out who sent me that card, but one thing I learned from this experience was that God truly does care about us. Not just as a nation, or a congregation, or as a family. He cares for us as individuals with our own separate needs and concerns. And when we reach out to Him, He will find a way to show us just how much He really cares.

HEADING HOME

My aunt was in the ICU, and from the reports I was hearing, things did not sound good. I called the hospital to check on her status, but there were no releases on file allowing them to share any information with me. All they could tell me was that if I wanted to see her, I should come soon.

I made a few phone calls to rearrange my afternoon plans, and then I headed toward the hospital. Having heard the reports from others, I was surprised to find her awake and talking. She spoke with me briefly, but then closed her eyes and went back to sleep.

In the past, I had heard that people can hear and understand you, even if they don't appear to be awake and alert. So I decided to have a heart-to-heart conversation with her. I stroked her hair and told her how I thought her time on earth was coming to an end. I mentioned all the loved ones in Heaven who were waiting for her. And then I told her not to be afraid. When she sees the bright light, she needs to remember that it is Jesus. She shouldn't be afraid of the light, but instead, reach out and take His hand.

She never opened her eyes, nor did she show any signs to acknowledge that she had heard me, but somehow I knew she had. I felt a peace inside, and knew I had done all I could to help her pass peacefully.

Later I called to check on her status. I was told that shortly after I left, a couple of loved ones were standing around her bedside. She had opened her eyes, sat up, waved good-bye, and then she was gone.

Hearing this sent a chill up my spine. They may have thought she was waving good-bye to them, but I knew the truth. She had been reaching out to take the hand of Jesus, just as I had encouraged her to do. I was so glad I had taken the time to go visit her. I hadn't realized how close she was to leaving this world, and it sounded like my visit had been beneficial in helping her to pass peacefully from this life into the next, holding the hand of her Savior.

HIDDEN TREASURE

As a means of keeping my young grandson entertained during church, I let him play with the case that held all my charge cards. It used to keep his older brother entertained for quite awhile. He would spend time taking the cards out and sliding them back in, sometimes even lining them up or trying to stack them.

However, the younger child didn't find it entertaining at all. He simply held onto the case and turned it over and over in his hands. He never even tried to open it. I'm not sure if he didn't know that it opened, or if he didn't care what was inside.

Suddenly it struck me as funny. If only he knew what was inside that case. With all those credit cards, he could go on quite a shopping spree. He could run up a bill in no time. He was holding an untapped treasure in his hands.

Being in church at the time, I couldn't help but make a religious connection. I thought about all the people who own a Bible, but never open it up to read what is inside. Oh, the hidden treasure located inside a Bible. It doesn't contain just words of wisdom, it contains words to live by. They are words that can guide us through any problem that we will ever face in life.

So go ahead and open your Bible. Dig deep into the treasure inside it. If the King James Version doesn't work for you, find one that does. I recently started reading the New International Version, and have found a new pleasure in reading my Bible. It is so easy to understand.

Don't deprive yourself of the hidden treasure inside that ageless book. It might just have all the answers you are looking for. And unlike the credit cards in my unopened case, you won't find any hidden fees or experience any financial repercussions! So open it up and dive in!

JUST WORDS

Walking through public places and listening to people talk can frequently be disheartening. The foul language people use is often just plain sickening. It used to be that words such as those were expressed only in the comfort of one's own home. Out in public places, people used to demonstrate a little more self-control and respect.

Some may think of them as just mere words. Just something you say when you are frustrated. Some might talk in that manner because they think it will impress others or show how bold they can be. To me, it all shows a lack of merit, vacant morals, and a blatant disrespect for the English language.

Words show the world, and everyone in it, what we are really like. They paint a picture of who we are inside. If we are foul mouthed and spit out angry, repulsive words all the time, we show everyone what wretched thoughts we harbor. Our polluted mouth doesn't necessarily impress people. It might not even strike fear in their hearts, if that is our goal. However, what it does do is to define us and clearly illustrate our character.

Words can make or break a person. They can help them get ahead in life, or they can bring them down into the gutter. And it is helpful to remember what the Bible says about words:

But I say unto you, That every idle word that men shall speak,they shall give account thereof in the day of judgment. For by thy words thou shalt be justified, and by thy words thou shalt be condemned.
Matthew 12:36-37

So when you speak, please remember that they are not 'just words.' The words you speak will make the difference between life and death, for you and possibly those around you. Now that's a lot to think about.

LEFTOVER APPLE PIE

It had been in the refrigerator for awhile, but it still smelled okay. I dipped a finger into it, and it tasted fine, too. I had made the apple pie for my husband, since it was a favorite of his. However, it had made its way to the bottom shelf of the refrigerator, and he must have forgotten about it. (It was probably too hard to bend over and look for it!) Since it still seemed okay, I decided to bring a piece of it to work with me.

At lunch time, I gingerly took a bite of the pie. I still wasn't convinced that it was okay to eat. However, bite after bite proved to taste fine. There was nothing that made me think the pie was not good. However, shortly after lunch time, my stomach began to feel sick, making me think I should have avoided eating it.

Why do we do this to ourselves? I wondered. In this case, I had literally filled myself with something that wasn't good for me. Then I realized we do this many times in life. We fill our minds with things that make our very soul sick. We watch TV shows that fill our minds with evil thoughts – shows about murder, adultery, homosexuality, and loaded with foul language, to top it all off. Perhaps society has accepted these things as a part of life, but that doesn't mean we should tolerate it. Not at all. In fact, we should strive hard to avoid it.

Then think about the things we fill our bodies with – soda, sugar, sweets and all kinds of junk foods that are not healthy for us. And yet we do it because it is easy. It's simple to pop open a can of soda, or grab a bag of chips and snack on it until we reach the bottom. But being easy shouldn't equate with being good.

We need to fill both our minds and bodies with things that are good, and healthy, and wholesome (just like the Bible tells us) and not allow ourselves to be conformed to the ways of the world. Just because it doesn't smell or have a bad flavor doesn't mean it's good for you. Even if it is just a piece of nice looking (but apparently rotten) apple pie!

NO PAT ON THE BACK

We had a busy weekend ahead of us. This was a holiday weekend and not only had I made family plans, but I had worked hard to organize an event for the kids in town. All week long, I had planned and prepared for this event. On Saturday morning, I had been up early to set everything up. In the afternoon, I had planned a trip to visit an elderly relative in a nursing home. Later, I took time to go out to grab a bite to eat with my husband, before returning home to make a pie and prepare for an Easter dinner with the family.

The next morning, I got up early to go help my daughter get her children ready for church. After church, we had our family dinner together with the kids and grandchildren, and then took a trip up to my parents' house to have some dessert with them. It had been a busy one, for sure, and one would think that having had so many successful events, I could have ended it on a happy note. But not so! On the way home, I had a spat with my husband over something that a little communication could have easily resolved.

So now I was feeling miserable. Not only was I very discouraged, but I came home to a messy house, with unpacked boxes from the town event, along with a sink full of dirty dishes. So I busied myself with the housework, and tried not to think about my problems. I would like to say that it worked, but it didn't!

At bed time, I found myself still very discouraged. Before going to sleep, I asked God if He could just give me a word of encouragement. After all the good things I had done over the weekend, I felt like someone should give me a little pat on the back to reassure me that I had done well. And then I fell asleep with high hopes.

However, in the morning I woke up just as disappointed. I had not had a very encouraging dream. Instead of feeling rewarded, I felt humiliated because I had done something stupid and embarrassing in my dream. So now I was feeling even worse than before I went to bed. I wondered why I couldn't even get some support in my dreams. After all, it was my brain that was creating them, right?!

As I got ready for work, I had a little talk with God. Not in a bossy or demanding manner, though. I told Him that if I were in charge, I would encourage people when they were down and out. In my situation, I would have sent an uplifting dream as a sign that what I had done was good and right, and that I didn't deserve to feel so beat up. But then I realized – who am I to tell God what to do?! He is the creator of the universe and everything in it. I am just one of a ka-zillion people who have walked across the face of His creation.

It made me think of Isaiah 45:9 that talks about the clay asking the maker what he is doing. I am just a messed up ball of clay, and God is the potter. I don't have the right to question what He is doing, or how, or why. I can't expect Him to jump when I want Him to. It is foolish for me to even think that way. I satisfied myself with knowing that some day I will be richly rewarded for all that I do that is right, or wholesome, or good, and then I went about my day.

The next weekend, I went to visit the same elderly aunt at the nursing home again. It was a beautiful day, and I thought she might like to get out for a bit. So we helped her into the car and took her to the playground to watch the kids play.

She was so happy to be outside and in a different environment. While the children played, we sat on the picnic table and visited. Suddenly, a beautiful Viceroy butterfly flew over and landed on my shoulder. I think it might have been a new butterfly, because it seemed quite fascinated with its wings. It just sat on my shoulder, opening and closing its wings like it was something new and exciting.

My aunt was absolutely fascinated. She sat there and smiled, watching this amazing butterfly, which seemed in no hurry to go anywhere. She said she wished she had a camera to take a picture of it. However, neither of us had the means to take a photo, so I observed as best I could from my angle, while she smiled and watched from hers. And finally, the little beauty just flew off.

After a time, I took her back to the nursing home and headed home myself. As I drove, I thought about last weekend and how I had longed for a pat on the back. I almost chuckled out loud when I realized that maybe I didn't get a pat on the back, but I did get a butterfly on my shoulder. God certainly has a way of making us feel special. It doesn't always come when we demand it, but in His timing, He does reach out to us with little rewards.

So God, thank you for the butterfly on my shoulder. It was just as rewarding as a pat on the back would have been (or maybe even better!)

NOT GOOD ENOUGH

Thankfully, it was just a dream (and not necessarily the one just mentioned in my last article. My brain just never stops, even when I am asleep!) Even though it was a dream, the emotions of feeling inadequate seemed to linger. No matter how much I tried to forget it, I just couldn't.

In my dream, I had worked extremely hard on a project for a friend of mine. It had been a massive project that had required a lot of man hours (or woman hours, in my case!) and I was pleased with the results.

I was so excited to show my friend, assuming they would be happy with the end product, too. However, my friend was clearly not impressed. Instead of thanking me for my hard work, they were displeased with the outcome and felt the need to do it over to their own liking. It left me feeling totally unappreciated, inadequate, and downright rejected.

My thoughts lingered on the dream all morning long. As I thought about it, I realized how God is not like the person in my dream. He is not human, and does not possess human likes and dislikes as we do. We don't need to work hard to impress Him, and then worry that He will reject our work, or even worse, make us feel inadequate.

God is always willing to accept the best that we have to offer. Maybe it's not as good as what someone else might have given, but the beautiful thing about God is that He knows our hearts. He knows if we are truly giving our best, or if we are just playing the game to put on a good show. And if we are doing all that we can and giving the best we have to offer, He is okay with that. He doesn't overlook our efforts, or decide to do things over because we didn't do it the way He would have.

So don't worry about not being good enough in God's eyes. He sees your efforts, and He knows your heart. You can't fool Him. If you are giving all you've got, even if it isn't as good as someone else, God knows that – and someday you will be richly rewarded for it.

PRIDE BEFORE A FALL

My husband owns a saw mill, but only uses it occasionally. When he has lumber to saw, he sometimes has trouble finding someone to help him. And he doesn't make enough money at it to be able to hire help. So occasionally I will lend a hand when he can't find anyone else.

Now I will be the first to admit that I am not a very muscular person. It has never been a part of my physical make up. When I was a kid, my uncle used to tell me I would disappear if I turned sideways because I was so thin. While I am not as thin as I used to be, I am still not powerfully built. However, I have never been one to run from a challenge, plus I don't mind helping my husband out when he needs it.

So he would saw the boards off, and I would drag them down the rails, turn them, and slide them out the side door. If I did it right, there wasn't much lifting to the job. Even though it was a physical task, I thought I was doing a pretty good job at this position.

One day while we were working, I started to feel a little pride welling up inside of me. For a scrawny female with no muscles, I was doing quite well at keeping up with my husband. In this moment of pride, I thought to myself, "I am doing a great job, just as good as any man could do!"

With that thought still fresh in my mind, I turned to throw a board out the side door and immediately lost my balance. I slid down the make-shift ramp of boards I had been building as I threw them out, and landed on the ground at the bottom. Realizing I had disappeared, my husband stopped sawing and waited until I climbed back up the pile and crawled back into the saw mill.

I brushed myself off, stood up, gave him an awkward smile, and then got back into position to go back to work. As I did, a verse in Proverbs came to mind:

Pride goeth before destruction, and a haughty spirit before a fall.
Proverbs 16:18

Well, I don't know about a haughty spirit, but I had definitely had a little pride effect going on. So in this situation, pride did come before a fall – and without delay! The thought had hardly passed through my mind when I was already rolling out the door! If God were that quick to correct us every time, there would probably be a lot less sin in the world!

THE HOLY LIFE

Walking across the parking lot on the way into work one morning, I was having a talk with God. I was telling Him how hard I have worked throughout my lifetime to live a holy life. I have avoided all the bad habits that can take control of a life – swearing, drinking, drugs, smoking, illicit sex. I didn't want to be controlled by a bad habit that had taken the reins and compromised the quality of my life.

As I chatted with God, I felt Him speak to me and say, "Not many people work that hard at living a holy life."

I knew He was right. (But then, naturally, He is always right. After all, He is God!) It is so easy to give into temptation in today's society. We are completely surrounded by evil traits, and even Christians are yielding. We find them giving up on their values and starting to blend in with the crowd. They believe God will still love them if they smoke, because God looks at their heart. Or God will understand if they slip and swear, because He understands that everyone is human and makes mistakes. And I'm sure that is true.

However, why not try to rise above all that? Why not climb to a higher standard and be the light at the top of the hill that shines brightly in an effort to show the way for other lost souls? After all, isn't that what God expects of us? Christians are called to be the light of the world, not to blend in and be hard to identify.

As far as I am concerned, the holier we can be, the better we will feel. I would rather strive to live a holy life and receive a greater reward in Heaven than to accept a lower standard of living and run the risk of being turned away at the pearly gates. I don't want to take chances with the opportunities I have been given and find myself missing out. This earth and life as we know it will someday pass away for each of us, but Heaven is forever. Do you really want to risk missing it?

THE PRESENCE OF LLOYD

It was Sunday morning, and my son and I were in church as usual. We sang songs about the presence of the Lord, and then he went to Children's Church while the pastor preached. After church, we socialized for a few minutes and then made our way out to the car to head home.

As we were walking across the parking lot, my young son tugged on my sleeve.

"There he is, Mom," he said, clearly in awe.

I looked around, trying to figure out who he was talking about. The only other person I saw was an elderly gentleman who sat in the back of the church every week. He was an usher, so he chose to sit beside the doors of the sanctuary to aid any latecomers with finding a seat.

Not understanding what my son meant, I simply asked, "Who are you talking about, sweetie?"

He pointed at the elderly gentleman and said, "Him."

I was still confused, and apparently my face showed it. But before I could question him further, my son looked up at me, with absolute admiration in his voice, and said "It's the Lord!"

A smile immediately crossed my face. I had no idea why he thought this man was the Lord, but he apparently was in reverence of him.

And then it hit me. His name was Lloyd. Apparently my son thought he was the Lord, and that he sat up back every week to monitor and observe our behavior!

I couldn't help but think how different things would be if the Lord did physically share His presence with us. We wouldn't gossip or talk badly about our friends, relatives, or neighbors. We probably would put more money in the offering plate. We wouldn't be so critical of things that didn't go our way. How different we would be if we could look over our shoulders and see that the Lord was watching us.

Well, Lloyd has since left us and gone on to his heavenly home. His chair now sits empty, but every time I look at it, I am reminded that we are in the presence of the Lord, and He is always watching over us, just as Lloyd oversaw our Sunday morning service week after week.

THE RAIN FALLS

One of the simple pleasures in life is lying in bed and listening to the rain fall. It has such a soothing effect. It's a natural relaxer. However, listening to the rain fall isn't as soothing to me as it used to be – not since the year we had so much rain that it caused a flood, which in turn washed our house away.

When things like that happen, it is hard to not question God and ask why. It naturally feels like a punishment, and we wonder what we did wrong to deserve such severe retribution. Some people deal with physical illnesses, some with fires, and some with the sudden and unexpected death of a loved one. Life can deal out some pretty harsh blows.

But there are a couple of Biblical principles to remember when we face those challenging times. Isaiah 43:2 tells us that God will be with us when we walk through the flood and flame. It doesn't say that He will spare us from it, but rather that He will stay with us.

The other thing to remember is how the Bible says the rain falls on the just and the unjust. We are all as human as the guy sitting next to us, and subject to the same human experiences. To expect God to shelter and deliver us from trials because we are Christians isn't proper thinking. Being a Christian doesn't exempt us from the challenges faced by the human race.

So when you are experiencing some pretty heavy rainfall, just think of how resilient a little blade of grass can be. It can get beaten down by the rainfall, but it always recovers and stands back up again. It knows it needs the rainfall (maybe not all at once!) so it sucks up the water, recovers from the downfall, and resumes the job it was called to do. May we all be just as resilient.

The storms of life will come, and not always as a gentle, soothing, washing rain. It will come as a downpour at times, and that is a guarantee. But my wish for you is that you will be as resilient as each blade of grass. Don't panic in the downpours. Just find solace in the rainfall, and know that God will give you the strength you need to make it through the storm.

THE RAPID RESPONSE

It was an unnerving situation, and I was not sure what to do about it. I found myself involved with a personal situation that I had never faced before, and the answer was obscure.

While on my morning break, I began exploring options, and trying to determine where to go from here. I composed a message to try to begin the process of seeking help, but then jammed it into a ball and threw it into the trash. I would need to process this a little longer to try to figure out what to do. I breathed a silent prayer, and then went back to work.

About an hour later, a coworker stepped into my office. We began a general conversation, discussing the weather and weekend plans. However, before the conversation was done, she had given me the answer I needed. Apparently she had already been though the exact problem I was currently facing.

After she left, I sat in stunned silence at my desk. Sometimes prayers take days, months, or even years to get answered. Sometimes they don't get answered at all, or not in the way we want them to. Yet this prayer had been answered in a matter of hours.

She may never know that she was an answer to my prayer. God used her to give me a piece of guidance and let me know how much He cared. I may not have known what to do, but He knew someone who was the voice of experience, and He had wasted no time in sending her my way! If only every prayer could be answered that quickly. Ah, but then we might get spoiled...!!!

THE ROCK

In church, we were singing a song about God being our strong rock. While we sang, I closed my eyes and envisioned myself holding onto this Rock. In my vision, I was stretched across a large, smooth surfaced rock, and it seemed that I was struggling to hang on in the face of the stormy winds.

That's when I realized that my vision wasn't correct. God is not a smooth surfaced rock that is challenging to grasp hold of. He is a rock with a precipice that is jagged and sharp enough to pierce the ferocity of the storm. Those jagged edges provide crevices and clefts that we can climb into to find shelter in the face of the storm.

Lately, it seems my family has been facing a series of storms which has extended over several years. There have been multiple trips to various Emergency Rooms. Some treks were due to injuries, whereas some have been more life-threatening, resulting in hospital stays or emergency surgeries.

One loved one had a significant blockage in an artery of his heart, and another required an emergency pacemaker placement. A couple of close relatives have been dealing with kidney failure, requiring dialysis three times a week. And of course, there are the battles with diverse types of cancers – breast cancer, lymph node cancer, skin cancer, and cancer of the esophagus.

We have always been a healthy family, yet we have had an unprecedented amount of illness and injury lately, and most of it is not anything we have brought on ourselves. Yet, one can't help but be concerned with what is still to come.

While I don't know for sure what the future holds, one thing I do know. There is a shelter in the Rock where we can be safe until the storms have passed. The storms will come, and they will go. And they may leave havoc when they have passed. But the Rock with its many crevices that keep us sheltered and protected will always remain the same. And that same Rock will be a firm foundation should we need to restructure our lives once the storm has passed. The Rock will always remain the same – strong, solid, unyielding, and sheltering for those who need a place to rest.

THE VOICE OF REASSURANCE

The original Snow White movie was playing at the theater for classic movie night, so I decided to take my grandson. He was only four years old, and I had fears that it might be too scary for him. However, my daughter and I decided we would give it a try. If he got scared, we would just leave early.

He was so excited about going to the movies, as I expected he would be. However, as I had also anticipated, he got quite scared at one point in the movie. He stood up, started putting his coat on, and said "I go home now." But before we had gathered our belongings, he changed his mind and sat back down. He decided if he sat in my lap, maybe he would be okay.

When it got to the part where the huntsman was going to kill Snow White, my grandson actually jumped. He quickly cover his eyes with both of his hands, afraid to see what was about to happen. I didn't want him to be afraid, so I leaned over and whispered in his ear, "It's okay, sweetie. He's not going to hurt her."

This was very reassuring to him. He relaxed, uncovered his eyes, and was actually able to make it through the rest of the movie.

As I thought about this the next day, it made me think of all the times when I was fearful or concerned about something that was happening in my life. Every time I turned to God, He has always been there to whisper softly in my ear and reassure me that everything is okay and He is always with me.

What would I do without that voice of reassurance? Like my grandson, my view of life might sometimes come from peeking through the fingers that covered my eyes, afraid to see what might be coming next. I thank God for that voice of reassurance, which will always speak softly to my soul and calm every fear I might face in life.

THRESHING OF THE WHEAT

Have you ever seen fields of wheat? I have not, but I'm sure it is an amazing sight. Why else would it have been included in one of our famous American songs, about fields of amber grain. Wheat is an important part of our lives and economy, not just beautiful to view.

The Bible talks about wheat in several places. It talks about wheat growing, being separated from the tares (or weeds,) and the chaffing of the wheat. I was thinking about the stages of wheat, and couldn't help but compare it to life and the stages we go through.

We all love the growing stage. When we are growing, life is good. We are learning and changing daily. Life is fun and exciting. There is so much every day that is new to see, and touch, and feel. Remember when you were a child and you came home so excited about something new you learned at school? And how disappointed you were to find out that your mother already knew it?! The growing stage is very exciting.

But then we reach maturity and life seems to slow done. We aren't growing anymore, and our stalk starts to turn brown. Does that mean our life has become stagnant? No, but it does mean we are about to be cut down. Should we be discouraged? Not at all. It's what we were created for. Wheat is useless standing idly in the field. If it isn't cut down and processed, it benefits no one.

The threshing process can feel painful, though. There is bumping and bruising, and harsh treatment as the chaff is separated. But that worthless matter has got to go in order to reach completion. The quality of the wheat would be compromised if the processing isn't thorough.

Sometimes we feel like we get stuck in the threshing stage of life. We feel like life is constantly processing us, even though we think we should have reached the refinery stage. The threshing seems to go on and on, even when we feel we can't take it any longer. That's when we need to stop and realize that maybe God has something more for us. Maybe He has a finer purpose for our lives, and He is allowing us to be processed to a greater degree to reach this higher level of perfection.

It might be a painful process, but what a blessing it will be to come out on the other side as the product God wants us to be. And don't forget that throughout the process, the hand of the Thresher is always there, supervising every step. He knows how to make a good product!

WHAT'S IN A SONG?

I was having a moment when life was getting the better of me. Things were not going well at work, and I was discouraged. I loved my job and the work I did, but I was struggling with some personality conflicts within the office, along with the constant changes that didn't always seem to make sense to me.

As I was driving home, I was fighting back tears. I had held this job for over a decade, and what I was going through just didn't seem fair. It seemed I should have earned some respect and status in my position, but that's not how it felt. To me, the whole situation was becoming unbearable, but I wasn't sure there was anything I could do about it. I needed my job.

The radio in my car was playing and, since it was December, most of the music was Christmas songs. But then my favorite secular song came on – "Soak up the Sun" by Cheryl Crowe. I love that song because it is so upbeat and encourages you to appreciate the simple beauties in life (like the sun!)

I turned the radio up and bellowed out the tune. I sang my heart out, like it was all that mattered in life. I put all my frustration and energy into singing that song. When it was over, I felt relieved and contemplated it for a moment.

My commute home is only a fifteen minute drive. With all the songs the radio station could have played during that time frame, they had played my all-time favorite one. It was like a little gift from God, just a small reminder that He sees my struggles and cares about what I am going through. And He knew just what to do to lift my spirits.

So what's in a song? Hope, encouragement, and renewal – just to name a few things. A message that says maybe tomorrow will be a better day, so don't dwell on the heartache of today. And a little blessing from God to show He cares.

WRESTLING WITH LIFE

Okay, so no one will argue that life is a challenge. We all go through times when it feels like we are struggling to keep our heads above water. Or here is a better scenario. Just picture yourself in a wrestling match. You are tired and exhausted, but you just don't want to give up. You finally feel like you are winning, when your opponent finds a burst of energy and throws you back on the mat. And sometimes, after being knocked down over and over, you feel like you just can't take anymore.

So when you get to that point and just can't handle one more moment of the struggle, remember the story of Jacob when he wrestled with the angel. It was a struggle that lasted all night long. It seems neither man was winning, but neither was willing to give up. Jacob ended up in pain, and walked with a limp after that battle, but he didn't give up until he got what he wanted. He wouldn't let go until he got his blessing.

Now there is a lesson for all of us in this story. We can be just like Jacob. When life keeps us struggling and we wrestle with it day after day, we don't have to give up. Hang on, and don't let go until you get what you want. Just like Jacob, keep holding on and wait for that blessing. It may not come today, and it might not come tomorrow. But rest assured, just as Jacob got his blessing, so will you.

As the Bible says in Galatians 6:9, "...in due season we shall reap, if we faint not." So keep wrestling with life, and wait for your reward. And remember the old saying that quitters never win!

ENDING THOUGHTS ON FOR THE SPIRIT

For many years of my life, I felt like I had failed God. As a teenager, God had placed a calling on my life. I thought it was to be in the field of music, so I applied to a religious college to get a certificate in vocals. I actually applied two years in a row, and was accepted both times. But when it came time to leave my family, I found myself unable to go.

We had always been a close-knit family, and I had only been away from home once that I could remember. I had gone to a week long Bible camp one summer, and had missed my family terribly. This college I had applied to was a fourteen hour drive away from home, and it was a year long program.

I truly wanted to go, and felt it was God's will for my life. It turned out that my brother-in-law had a sister who just happened to live in the same city as the college of my choice, and she had a spare bedroom available. She was very excited about the prospect of having someone from home come to live with her. To have it all fall into place so perfectly, it seemed like it must have been God's will for me.

So I took a trip to check the college out, and immediately fell in love with it. But it was in the city and I would need to take a series of buses to make my way to the college every day. That was scary to me, since I was just a country girl, but even more frightening was the fact that my family was so far away. In a moment of panic, I returned home and didn't pursue my calling.

A few years later, I married my high school sweetheart and we started a family. For the next few decades, I lived an average, mundane life. I was a stay-at-home mom, and eventually started my own child care center. I remained very involved in my church and community, but deep down inside, I always felt like I had failed God.

One year at Easter time, we watched a movie in church about Jesus and His disciples and the events leading up to the crucifixion. The movie showed how Peter stayed close to Jesus after He was arrested, how the cock crowed three times, and then it showed Jesus turning to look at Peter. In the movie, Peter fled in tears, realizing he had failed Jesus. I felt like sobbing right along with him. I could relate to his sense of failure.

Yet, I always had a feeling deep within me that there was more to life for me. I started keeping journals and recording things that happened in my life. I wasn't really sure what I would do with them, but it all seemed worth retaining. It seemed this information should be good for something. Then after my children were grown and out on their own, I started changing these memories into stories and writing books. Finally, my life made sense.

It's not that I had failed God in any way. I had remained true to Him throughout my lifetime, never wavering, never straying. It just took time to collect enough thoughts to create stories worthy of sharing. It was like everything in my life had finally come together and fallen into place. Looking back, I could see how He had been putting all the pieces of the puzzle together, and now I had a work (or works) worthy of sharing with others.

So with this book, I leave you with a few thoughts: Don't ever feel like God can't still make use of your life. As long as you have breath in your lungs, God can use you to further His kingdom. You may never be rich or famous, but there is something you can do. Search your heart and ask for His wisdom to find it.

And finally, once you reach your destiny, you will be able to look back and realize how God has paved the road for you to arrive there. God will never turn His back on you. If you remain true to Him, he will always be there to love, nurture, guide, and use you in anyway that you are willing to be used. Never give up in a spirit of defeat. It may take years (or decades, as was the case in my life) but you will get there.

Oh, and by the way, if you have read the New Testament, you may have noticed that Peter found his calling, too! Take care, God bless, and we'll see you someday in Heaven!

Acknowledgements

After writing a book such as this, one can't help but give credit to life (and the art of living it) as a main contributor. Without the flaws of life, we wouldn't develop character and become resilient or refined. Does life always go the way we want it to? Definitely not! Do we need to sit around and pout because it doesn't? No way! We just need to remember that we should always have a backup plan, and learn to laugh at what doesn't go according to our plans. Keeping a record of it and remembering to share the humor of the mishaps with those you love also helps.

As with my previous books, I owe a debt of gratitude to my sisters, Debbe and Linda, for their artistic talents and proofreading skills. And I wouldn't have been able to put this book together without the amazing computer skills of my niece, Michelle. Thank you, ladies! You are the wind that gives flight to my literary ideas. I may be the bird who was brave enough to step out of the nest and take a chance, but my family is the crosswind that keeps me airborne.

Above all, I thank God for giving me insight into the stream of life. He is the one who has taught me to not sweat the small stuff and learn how to turn what could have been a heartache into humor. He somehow helps it all make sense and gives life meaning, from start to finish.

OTHER BOOKS BY THE AUTHOR

Everybody has a bad day sometimes, but Mary Davis is having twelve of them – in a row! With a husband named Joseph, this couple knew Christmas would always be special to them. But packing twelve adult children and their families into one day of holiday fun proves to be less than joyful.

So Mary has come up with the perfect plan. She will invite each child to come home, one day at a time, thus stretching out the holiday season and avoiding the chaos of a houseful of not-so-holiday cheer. With a plan like that, what could possible go wrong?

But day after day of her holiday plan leaves Mary scrambling to try to save the day. With a resilient attitude (and the support of her faithful husband) she somehow manages to survive all twelve days.

***A Twelve Davis Christmas** is a comical view of a mother's love for her children, her efforts to give them her best, with a blend of Murphy's Law folded in. If anything can go wrong, it will happen to Mary and Joseph Davis – and their tribe of twelve.*

OTHER BOOKS BY THE AUTHOR

Abigail Carter would not deny that she had been blessed with three beautiful children. As a mother, her love for her children was as genuine as it comes. However, it seemed that recently someone had stolen her eldest daughter, Joy, and replaced her with a teenage nightmare. Then when her son, Corey, crashes his ATV into her brand new car and her youngest daughter, Holly, falls out of the tree and breaks her arm, Abigail knows she needs help. Keeping this family safe is beyond her human means.

Her husband, Russell, does all he can to help provide harmony in the family, but it just doesn't seem to be enough. Something has to be done for the safety of her children, and to maintain her sanity. So Abigail goes to the highest power she knows – right to the throne room of God.

At her request, God sends three angels to help out. But will these rusty humans have what it takes to keep them safe? At times, it seems like the heavenly trio has met their match with the three Carter children.

***Angels for Abigail** is a fun, fictional story of family trials and the heavenly visitors who are doing their best to try to keep the Carter children on track, safe from themselves, and out of trouble. But which trio will be the victors – the angels, or the kids they were sent to protect?*

www.ingramcontent.com/pod-product-compliance
Lightning Source LLC
Chambersburg PA
CBHW071518100726
47908CB00004B/1218

* 9 7 8 1 7 3 3 1 6 3 9 0 3 *